Richelieu Navigation Company

From Niagara to the Sea

The Finest Inland Water Trip in the World

Richelieu Navigation Company

From Niagara to the Sea
The Finest Inland Water Trip in the World

ISBN/EAN: 9783743442757

Manufactured in Europe, USA, Canada, Australia, Japa

Cover: Foto ©Andreas Hilbeck / pixelio.de

Manufactured and distributed by brebook publishing software (www.brebook.com)

Richelieu Navigation Company

From Niagara to the Sea

Official Guide, 1899

From Niagara to the Sea

The Finest Inland Water Trip in the World.

 • Illustrated •

Issued by the Passenger Department of the

Richelieu & Ontario Navigation Company.

228 St. Paul Street, Montreal.

OFFICERS
OF THE
Richelieu and Ontario Navigation Company.

Hon. L. J. FORGET, *President.*
C. F. GILDERSLEEVE, *General Manager.*
H. M. BOLGER, *Secretary.*
J. A. VILLENEUVE, *Accountant and Treasurer.*
GEORGE A. BROWNE, *Traffic Manager.*
H. FOSTER CHAFFEE, *Agent, Montreal.*
J. F. DOLAN, *Agent, Toronto.*
J. P. HANLEY, *Agent, Kingston.*
L. H. MYRAND, *Agent, Quebec.*

Entered, according to Act of the Parliament of Canada, in the year 1898, by
WM. A. DESBARATS,
at the Department of Agriculture.

Here, side by side, the Old and New
Has each a charm spread out to view:
From where Niagara's thunders roar
By scarped cliff and frowning shore;
In fertile fields and island groves,
By winding streams and wrinkled coves,
Its haunts of pleasure gay with life,
In scenes of peace and ancient strife.

From Niagara to the Sea.

NOWHERE on the continent of North America is there a more picturesque region than that which lies between Niagara and the sea. Niagara itself is one of the wonders of the world, with a fascination for all, and it is so easily reached from all directions that it is usually first visited by tourists who are desirous of seeing this greatest of Nature's marvels, and "doing" the grand tour of the famed Thousand Islands of the St. Lawrence. From all points south of the international boundary there is direct railway communication; nearly all the trunk lines of the United States converging at this great gateway to the tourists' paradise. Commencing at the Falls of Niagara, on the southern shore, then crossing Lake Ontario by steamer, or rounding its western extremity by rail, to Toronto, the Queen City of the West; embarking on one of the steamers of the Richelieu and Ontario Navigation Company, following the course of the lake, past the romantic waters of the Bay of Quinte, to Kingston, thence down the St. Lawrence, threading in and out of the Thousand Islands into the open stretch to Lake St. Francis, shooting the rapids, stopping over at Montreal and Quebec, and finally reaching the crowning glory of all, the incomparable grandeur of the Saguenay River.

Before civilization had changed the aspect of North America, **Niagara Falls.** the grandeur of Niagara was known to the inhabitants of the Old World; and

Whirlpool Rapids, Niagara Falls.

to-day, when the facilities of transportation have brought the most remote places within easy access, it is still regarded as Nature's greatest creation. The scene is much changed since the day when

Niagara Falls.

it was regarded as an object of superstitious fear by the Indians. Then, perhaps, its environment was more harmonious. Hemmed in by a dense forest, the approach to the Falls in those early days must have inspired a feeling of reference and awe. The only means of access was a narrow Indian path, but long before the majesty of the scene burst upon the spectator, the rumbling and crashing of its waters was heard, increasing with every step. No wonder that, to the Indian, Niagara was sacred, or that at stated periods pilgrimages were made to propitiate its anger. As an offering to the wrathful deity, a beautiful young girl was yearly bound fast in a canoe, and then set adrift in the rapids, while singers chanted her death-song till her frail bark was swept over the cataract, and swallowed up in the foam and spray beneath. Time also has left its impress on this inexplicable wonder. Slowly but surely the massive granite is being worn away by the unceasing turmoil of the waters, and, in 1850, a large portion of the Table Rock was precipitated into the gulf with a crash that was heard miles from the scene. Perhaps the best description that has ever been written is from the pen of Charles Dickens :— "At length we alighted; and for the first time I heard the mighty rose of

Victoria Park, Niagara Falls.

water, and felt the ground tremble underneath my feet. The bank is very steep, and was slippery with rain and half-melted ice. I hardly know how I got down, but I was soon at the bottom, and climbing, with two English officers who were crossing and had joined me, over some broken rocks, deafened by the noise, half blinded by the spray, and wet to the skin. We were at the foot of the American Fall. I could see an immense torrent of water tearing headlong down from some great height, but had no idea of shape, or situation, or anything but vague immensity. When we were seated in the little ferry-boat, and were crossing the swollen river immediately before the cataracts, I began to feel what it was; but I was in a manner stunned, and unable to comprehend the vastness of the scene. It was not until I came on Table Rock and looked— great Heaven, on what a fall of bright green water ! that it came upon me in its full might and majesty. Then, when I felt how near to my Creator I was standing, the first effect, and the enduring one—instant and lasting—of the tremendous spectacle, was Peace. Peace of mind, tranquility, calm recollections of the dead, great thoughts of eternal rest and happiness; nothing of gloom or terror. Niagara was at once stamped upon my heart, an image of beauty; to remain there changeless and indelible, until its pulses cease to beat forever.

N. F. P. & R. R'y Station at Queenston, opposite Lewiston, Brock's Monument in the Distance.

Oh, how the strife and trouble of daily life receded from my view and lessened in the distance, during the ten memorable days we passed on that enchanted ground! What voices spoke from out the thundering water; what faces, faded from the earth, looked out upon me from its gleaming depths; what heavenly promise glistened in those angels' tears, the drops of many hues, that showered around, and twined themselves about the gorgeous arches which the changing rainbows made. To wander to and fro all day, and see the cataracts from all points of view, to stand upon the edge of the great Horse-shoe Fall, marking the hurried water gathering strength as it approached the verge, yet seeming, too, to pause before it shot into the gulf below; to gaze from the river's level up at the torrent as it came streaming down; to climb the neighboring heights and watch it through the trees, and see the wreathing water in the rapids hurrying on to take its fearful plunge; to linger in the shadow of the solemn rocks three miles below; watching the river as, stirred by no visible cause, it heaved and eddied and awoke the echoes, being troubled yet, far down beneath the surface, by its giant leap; to have Niagara before me, lighted by the sun and by the moon, red in the day's decline, and grey as evening slowly fell upon it; to look upon it every day, wake up in the night and hear its ceaseless voice; this was enough. I think, in every quiet season now, still do these waters roll and leap, and roar and tumble, all day long; still are the rainbows spanning them, a hundred feet below. Still, when the sun is on them, do they shine and glow like molten gold. Still, when the day is gloomy, do they fall like snow, or seem to crumble away like the front of a great chalk cliff, or roll down the rock like dense white smoke. But always does the mighty stream appear to die as it comes down, and always from its unfathomable grave arises that tremendous ghost of spray and mist which is never laid; which has haunted this place with the same dread solemnity since darkness brooded on the deep, and that first flood before the deluge—light—came rushing on creation at the word of God."

Spot where Sir Isaac Brock Fell, at Queenston Heights.

Since the memorable visit of Dickens, the immediate vicinity of the Falls has been transformed. Beautiful parks form an agreeable setting to Nature's work. Hotels have been erected and bridges span the river. The region of the Falls, above and below, presents a series of delightful pictures that will claim the leisure of the visitor. One of the most picturesque spots, though comparatively seldom explored by tourists, lies between the Whirlpool and Queenston. The Niagara Falls Park and River Electric Railway affords an excellent opportunity of seeing the principal points of interest at a very moderate outlay. From Chippewa it closely follows the course of the river to Queenston, passing the Falls, the Whirlpool, and all the most picturesque and interesting spots of this region. Leaving Niagara, it is a short journey, either by rail or electric car, to **Brock's Monument.** the historic village of Queenston. The country here is particularly interesting. On the eminence is the monument erected by Canada in honor of Sir Isaac Brock, who fell during an engagement with the American troops on the 13th of October, 1812. From the gallery at the top of the column, reached by a spiral stairway, a fine panoramic view is obtained. On the opposite shore is the American village of Lewiston, and from the gorge above is seen the river as it comes foaming down, eager to end its struggles in the calm repose of the bay into which it spreads itself, sweeping on in serene grandeur to merge into the waters of Lake Ontario.

Niagara-on-the-Lake is twelve miles from the Falls—the surroundings are full of varied and historical interest—and possesses a really fine hotel in the Queen's Royal, under the same management as the Queen's Hotel of Toronto. It has become a very popular summer resort.

From Niagara we embark on one of the elegant steamers of the Niagara Navigation Company. These steamers run from Queenston

On Toronto Bay.

The Richelieu & Ontario Navigation Co.

down the Niagara River and across Lake Ontario. The sail occupies about three hours, and constitutes an ideal afternoon's outing. On **Fort Niagara.** the American point is Old Fort Niagara, which played an important part in the early history of the country. It was here that La Salle erected a palisaded store-house in 1678, when he was building the "Griffin," the first vessel, with the exception of a birch-bark canoe, ever launched on Lake Erie. This store-house,

Queen's Royal Hotel, Niagara-on-the-Lake.

after its destruction by the Indians, was rebuilt by the French in 1687, and finally a stone fort was erected on the site in 1749, by the Marquis de la Jonquière. Ten years later it was taken by the British, and remained in their possession until the close of the War of Independence, when it was ceded to the United States. As the steamer proceeds, the old fort is left behind, and soon the whole country, once sacred to Nature and the Indian, disappears from view. We are now in the stately waters of Lake Ontario, and our destination is Toronto. The broad expanse of water is a novelty after the turbulence of Niagara, while the cooling breeze is truly refreshing and invigorating. From the deck we are soon able to distinguish the shore to which we are heading; presently tall spires and massive buildings loom in the distance. The narrow strip of land which stretches out into the lake, and forms part of the natural harbor of Toronto, is Hanlan's Island, recently transformed from an unsightly strip of land into a picturesque pleasure-ground.

Government House, Toronto; Residence
of the Lieutenant-Governor.

Toronto. Toronto is beautifully situated on the north shore of Lake Ontario— the social, literary and educational centre of the Dominion, and one of the largest and most prosperous of its commercial centres. With environments of lovely natural scenery, ornamented with picturesque public parks, elegant and costly public buildings and private residences, and hundreds of stately edifices, Toronto rightly pre-empts the title of "Queen City of Canada," and to it annually is attracted that vast and largely increasing brotherhood whose quest is pleasure.

Few cities in the world are more admirably adapted for a summer resort than Toronto. Its situation on the lake, in the very heart of the temperate zone, is unsurpassed. It has a mild and equable climate, which renders the summer days pleasant. The average temperature in summer is between 10° and 20° hotter than that of the resorts of North Carolina and Florida in winter, and between 10° and 20° cooler than the temperature of those states in summer, while the elevation above the sea is about the same, and there is little

Trinity College, Toronto.

difference in humidity. The temperature is very near that of Denver, save that there is a greater daily variation in the latter city.

The site of this pleasant city, in the middle of the last century, was a trackless wilderness, the only inhabitants being a powerful tribe of Indians. In 1749, under the government of France, a trading post was established, bearing the name of Fort Rouille; not long after, the country passed into the hands of the British, and we do not hear much of what took place at Fort Rouille until 1793, and there seems to have been little change during the next half century. In 1792 Lieut.-Governor Simcoe arrived in the colony from England, and established his government at Niagara. During the following year, being dissatisfied with the location of his quarters, he set forth to select from the vast domain under his rule a site on which to establish a permanent seat of government worthy of the territory it was to represent. He had not far to seek, nor has the wisdom of his choice since been questioned. Crossing the lake, he was attracted by the advantages of the bay, as forming a natural harbor capable of meeting the greatest demands of commerce, advantages which had probably led the French to adopt it as a trading post, fifty years before, in opposition to the English post on the Oswego.

Monument in Queen's Park, Toronto, erected to Ridgeway Volunteers.

On landing, Simcoe pitched his tent near the shore, and soon a large body of men were clearing the forest and cutting roads. Simcoe named the city York, and remained for several months superintending the development of the infant capital. The first road that was cleared was Yonge street, connecting the seat of government with the Holland River, and opening up the waterway to the West. The residence of the Governor and Parliament buildings were established near the shore, and from this date, 1793, the city of York takes its birth.

There is little left in Toronto or in the neighborhood suggestive of its early history; the principal feature that recalls its memory is a massive granite boulder in the Queen's Park, bearing this inscription:

THIS CAIRN MARKS THE EXACT SITE OF
FORT ROUILLE, COMMONLY KNOWN AS FORT TORONTO,
AN INDIAN TRADING POST AND STOCKADE, ESTABLISHED
A. D. 1749, BY ORDER OF THE GOVERNMENT OF
LOUIS XV., IN ACCORDANCE WITH THE REPRESENTATIONS
OF THE COUNT DE LA GALISSONIÈRE, ADMINISTRATOR
OF NEW FRANCE, 1747-49.
ERECTED BY THE CORPORATION OF THE CITY OF TORONTO, 1878.

The administration of Simcoe was of brief duration; he was recalled to England in 1796, and little improvement was made under his immediate successors. Troublesome times were in store for the young city; its pioneers were early taught that security and independence were only to be obtained after bitter conflict. Early in the year 1812 a threatened invasion by the adjoining country turned all thoughts into the more serious channels of defence, and for nearly three years the city was under arms. An era of comparative peace appears to have followed, during which institutions were established, and the city placed again on the highway of prosperity. In 1834 the city was incorporated under the name of Toronto, but the seeds of internal strife were beginning to take root and threatened to plunge the community into all the horrors of civil war. The continued aggressiveness of the Colonial Government aroused the opposition to the point of rebellion, and an insurgent force was raised at the north end of the city that, for some days, menaced its security. Actual warfare, however, was prevented by the timely appearance of the militia, but discontent reigned for a long time, and it was not until a revision of the legislation of the

province took place that harmony was restored. In 1867 a new era dawned for the city; by the federation of the provinces Toronto became the capital of the Province of Ontario, which gave a great impetus to its commerce and substantially assisted in placing it in the proud position it occupies to-day. Another factor in the development of Toronto was the completion of the gigantic railway system of Canada, which has placed her in communication with the entire length and breadth of the continent. The site of the city is low,

Provincial House of Parliament, Toronto.

although it rises gradually from the water's edge to an elevation of over one hundred feet above the level of the lake. The streets resemble in arrangement those of the modern cities of the United States, and there is an up-to-date appearance about the whole city. The streets and avenues are broad and well paved, and, except on the principal business thoroughfares, have boulevards of well-kept lawns and shade-trees. To the stranger this is amongst the most pleasing features of the place, drives through the long forested avenues affording delightful glimpses of shrubbery and flowers.

The two main arteries of the city are Yonge and King streets, which cross each other at right angles. Starting from the foot of Yonge street, northwards from the bay, the most startling objects

School of Practical Science, Toronto.

seen are three fine buildings fairly typical of the city's wealth and enterprise—the Custom House, Bank of Montreal and Board of Trade. From this point radiate the wholesale business streets, whose massive structures may be seen on every hand. At the intersection with King the commercial hub of the city is reached. Above King, is an almost unbroken line of retail shops of every description, and it is perhaps the busiest of Toronto's streets. Yonge divides the city into two grand divisions, and is the great thoroughfare of the north, exceeding thirty miles to Holland Landing. King street is well built up with substantial stone and brick buildings, many of which are equal to any on the American continent. It is Toronto's Broadway. The residence of the Lieutenant-Governor, designed in the modern French style of architecture, is west on King. Near by are the old Parliament buildings, which are not interesting, except historically, and eastwardly, towards the bay, is the magnificent Union Station, utilized by the two great railway systems of Canada.

Another of Toronto's notable buildings, one which has attracted great attention, is the magnificent Temple, at the north-west corner of Richmond and Bay streets, erected by the Supreme Court of the Independent Order of Foresters, and in which are located the head offices of that great fraternal benefit society. The building, which is ten storeys high, and surmounted

The Pavilion, Horticultural Gardens, Toronto

by a central tower rising two storeys higher, is built of brown stone, brick, terra cotta and steel. It is a model of architectural and artistic construction and equipment, and is greatly admired by all who visit and inspect it. From the top of the tower, which is nearly two hundred feet above the street level, a magnificent view of the city, the surrounding country and Lake Ontario can be obtained, and on occasions the south or American shore and Niagara Falls can be seen. In the basement of the building are situated the safe deposit

The Temple Building, Toronto.

vaults of the Provincial Trust Company—the finest, largest and most thoroughly equipped vaults in Canada. Among the tenants are a bank and one of the largest publishing companies in the Dominion, and occupying eligible positions are the assembly halls and lodge rooms used by the order and by the Masonic fraternity. The building is practically fireproof; indeed, is the only building in Toronto in which fire insurance companies will place a certain class of risks.

The Exhibition Buildings are situated on the Garrison Reserve, at the west end of the city, overlooking Lake Ontario, and can be easily reached. They are ranked amongst the finest of their class in the world, and, especially during the holding of the annual

Toronto University.

exhibitions in September, attract large numbers of visitors. The Lunatic Asylum stands further to the north, on a level plain a large building, four storeys high, with a frontage of 644 feet and has, with the two adjoining hospitals, about 800 inmates. The Orphans' Home, Mercer Reformatory for Women, Home for Incurables, in Parkdale, Toronto's western suburb, are places worth seeing. Hyde Park, further west, is a magnificent stretch of alternate hill and shade, with beautiful trees and shrubbery, and it almost borders on the Humber, a delightful resort, west of which is Lorne Park. Rosedale, in the north-east, is adorned with fine residences, and its ravines are romantically picturesque, while Queen's Park, the Horticultural Gardens and other charming breathing places are found in the heart of the city.

The title of "City of Churches," to which Montreal and Brooklyn aspire, is also claimed by Toronto, and, in view of the multiplicity of sacred edifices, in endless variety of architecture, its right will not be disputed. St. James Cathedral, on King street east, said to have the highest spire on the continent, is a magnificent specimen of English Gothic architecture, and it is only one of a large number of stately and imposing edifices ; amongst others which may be mentioned, St. Michael's Cathedral, the Metropolitan (Methodist) Church, directly opposite, Jarvis Street Baptist Church, Congregational Church on Bond and Willow streets, St. Andrew's and Knox Presbyterian churches.

The Provincial Parliament buildings, at the southern end of Queen's Park, form a stately pile, which was erected at a cost of $1,250,000. It has a frontage of four hundred and thirty-five feet, with a depth of two hundred and sixty, and from its towers magnificent views of the city are obtainable. But a few rods away, in the western part of the park, is Toronto University, the pride of the city, which is said to be the only piece of collegiate architecture on the American continent worthy of standing room in the streets of Oxford. In its architectural features it belongs essentially to the Old World. The style is Norman, the proportions being noble and the harmony of the whole exquisite. The university was founded under a royal charter in 1827, and it has an endowment of $1,800,000. Its faculties include those of Arts,

The Island Park, Toronto

Science, Law, Theology and Medicine, and it is in federation with University College and Victoria University. It has also provision for residence, in this respect differing from most of the Canadian universities. The university proper, as in London and elsewhere, is a degree-conferring body, teaching being vested in the colleges.

Queen's Hotel, Toronto.

Near the university is the monument erected to the memory of the Canadian volunteers who fell while defending the frontier during the Fenian invasion of 1867.

Osgoode Hall—the palace of justice—where the highest courts of the province are held, claims attention while in this vicinity. Interesting is the exterior structure of this building, but its beauty is altogether eclipsed by the richness and elegance of its interior.

Another building, on Queen street, worthy of note, is the University of Trinity College, founded in 1852, and having an endowment of $750,000. Victoria University, much smaller than its sister, but architecturally a gem, and McMaster University, a grand-looking structure of brick and stone, are not far away, and other educational institutions worth visiting are the Baptist College, Wycliffe College, Knox College, the Normal and Model Schools, the School of Practical Science, etc. Visitors would also be interested in seeing the General Hospital, the Public Library, the Canadian Institute, with its museum and library, Victoria Hospital for sick children, Athletic Club, Armory, etc.

Toronto is well supplied with excellent hotels. The Queen's, one of the most comfortable hotels on the continent—possessing every modern convenience—has always been famous for its home-like comforts, and is in every way desirable as a family hotel. It is situated pleasantly, not far from either dock or station, yet quiet; a remarkably cool hotel in summer. It has been patronized by nearly all visitors of note to Toronto.

The Arlington has lately been coming to the fore as a less pretentious but thoroughly comfortable and well-managed hotel.

There are also numerous other hotels and private boarding houses. There is a capital street-car service, by which every part of the city can be reached, and a ride on the Belt Line will give the hurried tourist a fair idea of the city's best features.

The steamers for the Thousand Islands and Montreal leave the docks of the Richelieu & Ontario Navigation Company daily, except Sundays. Slowly they trace their difficult way among the fleets of small craft of every kind that swarm the bay, and point their prows towards the eastern outlet of the harbor, past Wiman's baths, on Hanlan's Island, and the new breakwater on the mainland side. On the north is the Don valley, issuing from the two converging Rosedale ravines, which, in their solitary grandeur of stupendous depth and lofty pine within their fold, remain the monument of some primeval drift. In front is the island, which protects the harbor from the boisterous weather of the lake, extending its narrow strip of land almost across the entire breadth of the city. Upon the surface of the bay can be seen the almost incessant movement of shipping vessels, the island yachts, with their gracefully bulging sails, and canoes and skiffs dotted here and there among the larger craft. The whole scene is an imposing one, and the spectator is content to watch with the growing enchantment which increasing distance lends, until the picture grows dim before the eyes and fades from view in an indistinguishable haze.

After issuing from the narrow strait into the broad expanse of blue waters that stretches far beyond the reach of human vision, the stately vessel, instinct with the power of her mighty enginery, rapidly forges ahead, and her ponderous wheels are felt to quicken their pulsations as, gathering strength, she strikes with vigorous strokes into the placid bosom of the lake.

Richelieu & Ontario Navigation Co.'s Steamer "Toronto."

The new and beautiful steamer "Toronto," built at Toronto during the past year, will begin her regular trips on the Toronto-Montreal route on June 1st, and will sail from Toronto every Tuesday, Thursday and Saturday. This magnificent boat has spacious and elegant passenger accommodation, including one hundred and forty staterooms, four parlors and large Pullman sleeping cabin, and has a sleeping capacity for four

Steamer "Toronto."

Port Hope, Ont.

hundred and thirty passengers. The dining room, situated on the upper deck, has a seating capacity for over one hundred persons.

The interior finish and decorations and the spacious halls and deck saloons are most elaborately executed, the main and gallery saloons being finished in Francis I. Renaissance, with the dining room in Louis XVI.

The entrance hall, on the main deck, is decorated in Neo-Grec, with modern Renaissance details, with the smoking room in Oriental treatment. The refreshment, writing rooms and barber shop are in Elizabethian panelling of *prima vera*, natural wood finish. The main staircases are in Honduras mahogany, with wrought metal balustrades in hammered leaf work, finished antique bronze, the main newals carrying bronze figures supporting electric torches.

To give some idea of the dimensions of this modern and fine steamer, a few figures would not be out of place. The length over all is 278 feet, width of beam 62 feet, depth 14 feet. The engines are of the triple expansion class. The feathering paddle-wheels are

22 feet outside a id 10 feet 3 inches face of bucket. The average time-table speed will be 17 miles an hour, with a capacity for 20 miles when required, which permits of more convenient hours of sailing being arranged for than heretofore.

The first port of call for the steamer "Toronto," after leaving the city of Toronto, will be the pretty little village of Charlotte,

Charlotte, N. Y. N. Y., lying on the southern shore of Lake Ontario, some seven miles north of the city of Rochester, and one of the best points of embarkation for the Thousand Islands trip, and, on returning on the western trip, calls at this port on Sundays, Wednesdays and Fridays, while other steamers of this popular line call at Cobourg and Port Hope on alternate days.

Charlotte itself is a pleasant and picturesque village, situated at the mouth of the Genesee river, and is the lake port for all the tourist business converging in the city of Rochester. The environments of Charlotte contain a great many attractive resorts, such as Ontario Beach, just below Charlotte, and connected with Rochester by a branch of the New York Central, and during the summer season trains run back and forth at frequent intervals. Good fishing and hunting are plentiful in the immediate vicinity, and bathing, boating and driving, interspersed with social attractions at the summer hotels, cannot fail to interest and amuse the traveller. Other favorite places in close proximity to Charlotte are Windsor Beach, Lake Bluff, Sea Breeze, Irondequoit Bay, etc.

Rochester is regularly laid out, with well-paved streets, bordered with shade-trees. It has earned the title of the "Flower City,"

Rochester. from the numerous nurseries situated there, which, with the seed-farms during the season of bloom, are gorgeous sights, covering acres with their brilliant flowers. Rochester is noted for its many fine buildings and private residences. The University of Rochester, an educational institution, is a fine structure, built of red sandstone.

Caught near Belleville, August 31st, 1880.
Total weight, 117 lbs.

Yacht Racing on the Bay of Quinte.

surrounded by extensive grounds beautifully laid out. The Falls of the Genesee river (three in number) are among the natural attractions. Rochester is an important railroad centre; the trains of the New York Central, Lehigh Valley, Buffalo, Rochester & Pittsburg, New York, Lake Erie & Western, and Western New York & Pennsylvania railroads all connect at this point. Connections are made between Rochester and Charlotte by means of the New York Central trains; also by Electric Railway. Leaving Charlotte, the steamer sails down Lake Ontario, on her way towards Kingston.

On Tuesdays, Thursdays and Saturdays the Richelieu & Ontario Company's steamers pass through the Bay of Quinte on their westward trips.

The steamer speeds on past shores filled with the mystery of unwritten history, for already in the distance the dim outlines of the lighthouse of Port Hope may be seen, and our footsteps may soon press—

> where, centuries ago,
> The red man fought and conquered, lost and won.
> Whole tribes and races, gone like last year's snow,
> Have found the eternal hunting grounds, and run
> The fiery gauntlet of their ancient days.

Here, though largely shrouded in mystery, were fought the fiercest and most relentless battles for the possession of the midland region of Canada. The territory was well worth fighting for. It is the fabled "happy hunting ground"; deer, black bear, lake salmon, sturgeon, bass and lake-trout were found in lavish abundance, and still amply repay the skill of the sportsman ; and wild rice and maize grew over vast tracts. No wonder, then, that Huron and Algonquin struggled valiantly, though unsuccessfully, to retain possession against the attacks of the Iroquois, that race of athletes who lorded it over half a continent, and whose alliance was eagerly courted by France and England.

A few miles inward is the Indian settlement of Hiawatha, named after the Hercules of the Objiway mythology, whom Longfellow has immortalized in his melodious trohaics. Here we may wander by the "groves of singing pine-trees, ever singing, ever sighing," and perchance follow in the trail trod centuries before by moccasined feet or black-robed priest. How changed the aspect : the struggles for supremacy are ended, and the old tragic scenes are rapidly passing into the twilight of Homeric legend.

The prosperous town of Port Hope once bore the Indian name of Ganaraske. The town is most picturesquely situated on the north shore of the lake, rising in the background to a noble

Port Hope. eminence, rendering it one of the most healthful of residential situations. To the sportsman it is a paradise, as from its position it is the gateway to the sporting territory of the region.

The next stoppage is six miles further along the coast, at Cobourg (5,000), a town of considerable business activity, it being

Trenton, Ont.

the distributing centre of an exceedingly fertile portion of the Province. It is a place of no mean pretensions to beauty, its streets being broad and neatly laid out, as well as frequently adorned by elegant public and private buildings. The drives along the eastern approaches of the town are very beautiful.

Cobourg.

Soon after the steamer leaves Cobourg, the day is drawing near to a close, and the voyage acquires a fresh interest for the mind that

Bridge Street, Belleville.

is responsive to the picturesqueness of nature. The western sun is setting, with its great halo of crimson light, behind the Northumberland hills; eastward, the clouds that hang like the filmy draperies in heaven are roseate from the setting sun, while towards the south and east, Ontario's waters, stretching far away into the grey horizon, reflect the splendor of the sunset scene from their imperial bosom, until the view slowly dissolves itself, and the shadow of the coming night begins to brood upon the face of things.

Darkness creeps along the distant reaches of the deep, and possibly the moon, full-orbed or crescent, comes to shed its luminous rays upon the dark watery pathway of the great steamer, as she moves along the coast of Prince Edward County, past the docks, down towards the lower gap which opens into Kingston, the next stopping point.

While she is plying her midnight way into the early hours of the morning, we shall leave her, with all her slumbering passengers, to

Bay of Quinte. trace a very pleasant detour through the Murray Canal and Bay of Quinte, available to tourists by means of the Richelieu Company's steamers "Hamilton" and "Algerian," which alone take this route down, whereas the other steamers take this course on their return trip on Tuesdays, Thursdays and Saturdays.

The steamer takes a circuitous course from Cobourg to its next stopping place, Brighton, passing in the distance on the right the Sandbanks, the Scotch Bonnet light and Weller's Bay. After rounding the Presque Isle light into the bay of the same name, it has to trace a devious way among the difficult and intricate channels, buoyed up by a system of range lights to facilitate navigation among its shoals, until finally the port of Brighton is reached. This has a well-sheltered harbor, and is a district of considerable industrial activity, its manufactures covering flouring and plaster mills, a tannery, and canning works.

From Brighton the end of Presque Isle Bay is crossed to the Murray Canal, which has been constructed across the narrow isthmus that joins the Prince Edward peninsula to the main land. This canal has been the means of opening up for a highway of steamboat traffic the sinuous picturesqueness of the Bay of Quinte, with its splendid scenery of elevated shore, capped by tall trees, and of long reaches which give the place a romantic beauty eminently fitting it for a field of summer pastime and recuperation. We cannot issue from the narrow waters of the canal, with its four spanning

Forrester's Island Park.

bridges (railway and three highway bridges), into the broader waters of the Bay of Quinte, without allowing our thoughts to drift back to the heroic Fénelon, brother of the famous Archbishop of Cambray, who, in 1668, directed his steps into the heart of these solitudes. Reared amid the refined luxury of his ancestral home in Périgord, with the prospect of the alliance of his house with one of the most powerful families of France, there is a tinge of romance mingled with his deeds. But as we peruse the narrative which

Glenora, Ont.

history has preserved of the struggles, privations and dangers to which he was exposed in extending the cause of religion, terminating with his life, at the early age of thirty-eight, the romantic spell is broken, and there gathers around his memory the aureole of martyrdom.

Leaving the Murray Canal, the steamer courses along the south shore, past Indian Island, over to Trenton (5,000), at the mouth of the River Trent. This is at once the centre of a fine agricultural district and the home of vigorous and varied industries, which are favored by the presence of exceptional water power and the distributing media of the Grand Trunk Railway and the steamboat lines. The town has a beautiful and commanding site at the head of the Bay of Quinte, of which it has the sweep clear up to Belleville. On the west it is flanked by the sister mounts, Pelion and Ossa, from whose elevated summits the low-

Trenton.

lands and the bay, with its beautiful indentations of coast line, stretch before the eye in splendid panorama. Northward, the eye can catch, amid the undulating hills of Sydney and of Murray, the gleaming waters of Trent's meandering stream, while southward, beyond the bay and peninsula as far as the sight can reach, lies Lake Ontario's boundless blue, the waters of an inland sea.

From the canal, the Central Ontario Railway trains run to Consecon, seven miles east, where there is excellent bass and pickerel fishing, and to Picton, in the vicinity of which anglers will find fair sport.

If the trip, however, is to be continued uninterrupted, on leaving Trenton, the steamer passes Baker's and Nigger's islands on the left down the bay towards Belleville. On the right is Rednersville, the principal shipping port of the townships of Ameliasburgh and Hillier, well known for their fruit industries. Their apple and grape production is exceedingly progressive, both in quantity and quality.

In the distance over our bows looms up by this time the long and graceful span of Quinte Bridge, which is said to be the longest highway bridge in America. To the left, before the bridge is reached, the Provincial Institution for the Deaf and Dumb is seen. As we near the massive bridge, its ponderous draw is opened at a signal from the steamer's whistle, and we glide swiftly through the opening of the graceful structure, which, from the distance, seemed to present an impassable barrier to our progress.

Entering the harbor, the eyes rest upon the city of Belleville (population 11,000), the county town of Hastings, at the mouth of the Moira river. A

Belleville.

Martello Tower, Kingston.

brief glance at the situation and surroundings of the city is sufficient to convince the tourist or sportsman that nature has singled out this spot as an ideal summer resort. Far out in the open waters, or winding in and out along the shore, hidden among its coves, are a series of camping and fishing grounds, the discovery of which will fill the sportsman with delight. Here, amidst an infinite variety of scenery, and the enjoyment of rare and pure atmosphere, for which the district is famous, the pleasures of boating and yachting may be indulged in to the heart's content. This is the prospect presented to us before we set foot on the shores of the city commonly known as the "Beautiful." From any elevated site its claim to this title will be found justified. In the centre of the valley, through which the River Moira flows to the bay, is the business part of the city, with its substantial buildings and well-ordered streets, picturesque even in its thoroughfares. On the hills, which rise gradually from the vale, are scattered the modern and beautiful homes of its citizens, amid shrouded nooks and retreats, combining the pleasures of rural life with the advantages of a thriving city.

Belleville boasts of a number of fine public buildings, the most noteworthy of which are the Court House, the Armory and Drill Hall, the Post Office, City Hall, and other Government buildings, and the Carman Opera House. The principal seat of learning is Albert College, a group of buildings comprising chapel and class rooms, dormitory and professors' residence, gymnasium and museum of natural history. The other leading institutions are the High School, the Ontario Business College, Belleville Business College, and the Ontario Institution for the Deaf and Dumb.

The steamer crosses over the bay to Belleville's charming summer resort, Massassaga Point, which contains a first-class hotel and several cottages, and is set in the midst of a scene of unequalled beauty. Besides being in the centre of the haunts of the maskinongé, it provides for every kind of amusement.

Leaving Massassaga Point, the steamer enters an expansion of the bay, across which she traverses past Ox Point and Point Ann, with their inexhaustible limestone quarries, and Big Island. To the right is the village of Northport, the shipping place of the township of Sophiasburg, a district which produces large quantities of apples, cheese and hops.

Moving on eastward, Telegraph Island is passed, with its lighthouse, Peterson's Ferry on the right, and on the left the Mohawk Indian Reserve of Tyendenaga, a territory which the white intruder left to the ancestral owners of the whole land. It is populated by the Six-Nation Indians—Mohawks, Oneidas, Onondagas, Senecas, Cayugas and Tuscaroras—remnants of the intrepid Iroquois, who left the main stock of their people in New York, in 1784, and came to Canada. Here they have settled down in peace, while the white man, with his rushing railways and his noisy manufactories, is

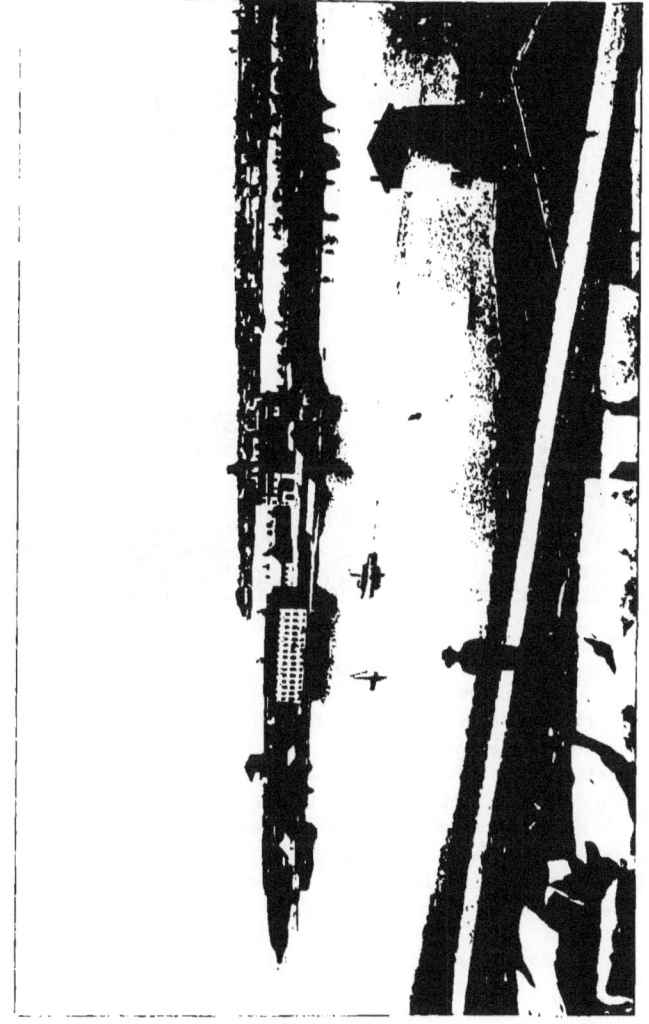

The Military College and City of Kingston.

rapidly obliterating the traces of his old hunting grounds in the principal solitudes which stretched along the margin of the great lakes. They are a Christian community, as is attested by the grey spire of the church, that can be seen from the bay, lifting its head above the clustering trees. A gift to which the Indians point with pride is a silver communion service presented to them by Queen Anne, carefully preserved and loyally cherished. In many ways

Alexandria Bay, Thousand Islands.

they show exceptional gifts, especially in the line of practical arts, such as needlework, for which the Mohawk mothers are famous. Even the children show a natural skill in drawing, in which they evince a decided superiority over white boys of the same age. The men occupy themselves either at agricultural pursuits or in the employment of some of Deseronto's manufactories.

Nearing the docks of Deseronto, the steamer passes Forester's Island Park, owned by Dr. Oronhyatehka, a pleasant summer resort, commanding an extensive view. This island was part of the domain of the powerful Mohawk chief whose name is perpetuated in the busy port we are now entering.

Deseronto is conspicuous from the distance by the massive lumber piles, the tall smoking chimneys from the numerous large factories, some brick-colored and some of the color of zinc; by the dockyards, with the steamers and vessels in process of contruction or repair, all giving a prepossession to the spectator that this is surely a place of great industrial activity.

Deseronto.

The town is built on a hill which rises gradually from the water's edge northwards. Situated on an elbow of the bay where the Belleville Reach abruptly turns from the north-east to south into the Picton Reach, it has a survey of the beautiful scenery of both, as well as, towards the east, of the tortuous channels of the Napanee River. Towards the west, the Telegraph Island light looms up in the misty distance, like a fairy tower floating on the water's surface ; towards the south, the long stretch of elevated coast, clothed in foliage green, seems to approach so close to the opposite shore, away ahead, as to leave apparently only a narrow gorge between, through which, now and then, appear the sails of yachts and schooners working up the Reach.

Crossing the Long Reach for Picton, on the picturesque shores of Prince Edward county, the passage is enhanced by the beauty and variety of the scene which greets the eye. The entry to Picton Bay, enclosed by two lofty shores, is impressive, lending beauty to the prospect of the town, which is now in full view. From the elevation of these shores, a marvellous stretch of lake and woodland grandeur is seen. Owing to the sheltered position of its harbor, Picton is highly favored as the shipping centre of Prince Edward county. Fruit and grain are grown in abundance in this region and distributed from Picton. It is a manufacturing town of importance, having large canning factories, foundries, and a shipyard for the building and repairing of vessels. It is also the terminus of the Central Ontario Railroad.

Picton.

Thousand Islands Scenery.

The town is provided with all modern improvements in the way of water works, electric light, fire alarm, telephone and telegraph systems. The drives on either side of the town are very fine, the roads being excellent and tracing a way among rich farm-lands, splendid orchards, rural homes and beautiful inland lakes, as they near the shores of Lake Ontario.

About ten miles from Picton, on the lake side of Prince Edward county, are the Sandbanks, mounds of shifting sand on the margin of the great lake, a strange and interesting scene, in a region of historic importance, for near here, in 1668, the Kente mission was established.

On leaving Picton the steamer courses along the shore in the direction of Glenora, where the land rises abruptly to an elevation of nearly two hundred feet. Huddling at the foot of the mountain, with scarcely room for a footing, are the Glen House, for tourists, extensive flouring mills, foundry and machine shops, deriving their power by water carried through a narrow pipe from the lake on the summit of the cliff, the celebrated Lake on the Mountain. It is a little circular sheet of blue water, nestling like an alpine lake among its trees in cosy solitude. There is a romantic beauty about this lake, as well as a tinge of mystery. Being on a level with Lake Erie, and with no apparent inlet, it is supposed to be connected with it by means of subterranean channels. Clear and crystal are its depths, which remain unfathomed, an ideal spot around which to weave dainty stories that may vie with the beauty of classic legend.

The view from the summit of the mountain is enchanting. Across the stretch of water lie the pleasant camping grounds and cottages of Dingman's Island. To the right is the cataract that overleaps the edge of the mountain into a romantic chasm, near the base of which is a well-known cave. Leaving this delightful spot, we arrive at the historic Adolphustown, with its beautiful memorial chapel which perpetuates the memory of the United Empire Loyalists, a body of sturdy men so named from their devotion to the British Crown during the Revolutionary War. It was through their efforts that this district was settled after the close of hostilities in 1812.

Interesting and varied scenery meets the eye as we take in the surrounding prospect. To the left is Fredericksburg, and just beyond Prinyea's Cove, a favorite mooring ground for yachts, furnishing excellent sport in the form of pike fishing, and also affording a safe harbor in the event of storm. Two miles further on, jutting out into the bay, is Indian Point. Its gravel beach is formed by the washings of the waves coming in from the Upper Gap, the waters of which separate Prince Edward county from Amherst Island, and make a channel between the bay and Lake Ontario. A dense grove of cedar covers part of the shore, making it a desirable camping ground.

The steamer now issues out upon the waters of the Upper Gap, and again we catch sight of endless blue over our starboard. Behind us lie the jutting headlands of Quinte, backed by the dark-green hills of Glenora down the Adolphus Reach. Over our quarter is the coast of Amherst Island, which we are rapidly approaching, as we point our bow for the North Channel, which separates the island from the mainland on the north. Around us roll the slow swells of the lake, barely making themselves felt in the slight undulatory motion of the vessel. Here and there, upon the water, can be seen the graceful forms of white gulls careening on the waves. As we approach they lift successively on their narrow crescent wings, perform a mazy tracery of motion in mid-air, crossing and recrossing one another, circling and intercircling in mystic figures, until they again alight in the distance upon the rolling water.

A Group of the Thousand Islands

On the right, as we pass into the North Channel, is Emerald, the upper landing of Amherst Island. It is the port of a prosperous agricultural district, and the home of an old artist, Daniel Fowler, whose achievements in landscapes and still-life representations have won him considerable praise.

On the mainland shore, a little further on, is the village of Bath, formerly known as Ernesttown, one of the oldest places in the district.

The next port of importance is Stella (Amherst Island), twelve miles west of Kingston. It is a place not only of brisk industries in the agricultural line, but is a most pleasant summer resort, with its picturesque and sheltered bay. There is a large summer hotel on **Stella.** Stella Point for accommodation of tourists, and the fishing grounds are excellent. It is a convenient as well as a pleasant retreat, by reason of its neighboring supply stores, cable communication with the mainland, daily mail and steamboat service. The drives about the island are beautiful.

The steamer now steers a clear course for Kingston, past the Three Brothers Islands, at the foot of Amherst, and Salmon Island, across the broad waters of the Lower Gap, leaving the picturesque Bay of Quinte finally behind.

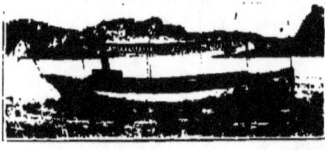

Launch built by the Davis Dry Dock Co. of Kingston.

Proceeding along the north shore, we see the village of Cataraqui, adjoining which is Kingston's "city of the dead," where repose, among its silent tombs, the remains of the celebrated Sir John Macdonald, Premier of Canada, and Sir Alexander Campbell. Farther on is the village of Portsmouth, distinguished for its ship-building industry and trans-shipping facilities. Here also are located the Kingston Penitentiary, the Rockwood Asylum, and the Church of the Good Thief.

And now we are at Kingston, the Woolwich or West Point of Canada, with its Military College, its massive grey stone forts, its **Kingston.** Martello towers and imposing public buildings. It is beautifully situated at the foot of Lake Ontario, at the head of the River St. Lawrence, and at the mouth of the Rideau or Great Cataraqui River, which, with the Rideau Canal, connects it by water-way with Ottawa. A settlement was begun here by the French, under Governor de Courcelles (1672), with the name of Fort Cataraqui, for the purpose of protecting the fur-traders from the murderous depredations of the Indians. His successor, Count de Frontenac, built a massive stone fort, giving it his own name, which still attaches to the county. This fort was alternately seized and occupied by the French and English, until it was destroyed by the latter, under Colonel Bradstreet, in 1758. It was again rebuilt under the name of Fort Henry, which it retains to-day. At the time of the union of Upper and Lower Canadas (1841), Kingston was made the capital, but the seat of government was afterwards removed to

Montreal (1841), and afterwards, in turn, to Toronto and Kingston, until, in 1859, Ottawa was chosen as the permanent capital by Her Majesty Queen Victoria.

At Kingston vessels constructed for lake navigation only, transfer their cargoes to barges and river boats for conveyance to Montreal, while in turn these tranship their cargoes, brought from Montreal, to the lake boats.

Kingston has quite extensive industries in ship-building and ship repairing, it carries on an extensive grain trade, and has large smelting works for extracting metal from the ore.

It is also a great educational centre. Its colleges are of continental repute. They are Queen's University, Royal Medical College (for male and female), Royal Military College, School of Gunnery, School of Art, Science Hall, School of Mining, Kingston Business College, Congrégation de Notre-Dame, St.-Mary's-on-the-Lake Convent, and Kingston Ladies' College, and several smaller institutions.

The general appearance of the city is that of solidity and antique beauty. Its prevalent limestone architecture has secured for it the name of the "Limestone City." It is well laid out, and here and there is adorned by massive buildings, such as the City Hall, Court House, with its pillars and dome in Grecian Ionic style, Custom House, Post Office, St. George's (Anglican) and St. Mary's (R. C.) cathedrals, which latter are accredited with being the finest churches of Canada west of Montreal; in fact, the tower of St. Mary's, as recently rebuilt, is a masterly monument of Gothic architectural art, and will eminently repay personal inspection by the tourist. The city is provided with a well-appointed electric street railway, which

In the Thousand Islands.

adds to its general comeliness as well as to its conveniences. It has good hotel accommodation.

We launch out at early morn upon the silent bosom of the majestic St. Lawrence. Behind us lie the cold grey structures of the Limestone City, with its domes and pinnacles bathed in the rising lustre of the morning sun. Towards the **Thousand Islands.** south-west stretches the vast calm surface of Ontario, beyond the gap, dimmed by the lifting mist, and bearing on its bosom the shadowy outline of a distant ship. Across the river stands Garden Island, with its cluster of shipping, and City View Park, on Wolfe Island, with its undulating groves. Before us lies the entry to the sinuous channels of the famous archipelago of the *Thousand Islands.*

Fiddler's Elbow—Lost Channel—Canadian Islands.

These commence near Kingston with Wolfe, the largest of their number, where the waters of Lake Ontario issue into the broad channel of the St. Lawrence, and extend down to Brockville, a distance of some fifty miles. They number, in all, some seventeen hundred, varying in size, shape and appearance, from a small lump of barren rock projecting from the surface of the river, to the large fertile area of land, crowned with richest foliage and lofty trees, and ornamented by neatly colored summer residences, or left in their primeval rudeness. As we wind in and out amid these charming islands—sylvan gems which deck a crystal stream—the rapidly changing picture almost bewilders us. Delightful, indeed, would be a short vacation spent in their midst. Here we could

Leave the town with its hundred noises
Its clatter and whirr of wheel and steam,
For woodland quiet and silvery voices,
And a forest camp by a crystal stream.

The picture is too vast for us to be enabled to unite it into one grand scene, its devious water-courses sometimes opening into swelling lakes, or closing into narrow gorges across which the shadow of the island trees throw their image ; with their clustering groups, head above head, like Neptune's flock asleep ; with their prodigality of decorative coloring, both from the hand of man, in neatly ornamented cottages, and from the more artistic hand of nature, in her mosses, lichens, flowers and the arabesque of dark in-woven leaves, penetrated by the radiance of the pale blue sky ; but most of all with their shifting kaleidoscope of scenes which throng the vision as the steamer traces its way among the labyrinthian channels. Here and there the course seems completely closed, and we think the boat must back out, when nearer approach to the moss-grown shores discloses a hidden outlet by a sudden turn, perhaps into a sheer-sided rock-bound strait, whose shores we can almost touch from the decks, or into a beautiful amphitheatre of lake, bounded by myriad isles. Their scenery has, indeed, more of the element of the beautiful and pretty, which wins the spectator by its delicate and varied loveliness, than of the sublime which holds our minds in awe and reverence before the power of majesty or of size. Their uniqueness is not in their grandeur, but in their daintiness of tints, of shifting scenes, of growing and dissolving views, of land-locked bays and lakelets, and sinuous transparent streams that wind and intersect in wildest tracery. They are the nearest approach, perhaps, that the world presents to the realization of the ancients' dream of the *Fortunæ Insulæ*, the embodiment of ideal beauty of garden-land and stream.

These islands were the scene of several thrilling and romantic adventures during the days of the rebellion. The burning of the "Sir Robert Peel" occurred here in 1838, by a band of outlaws headed by "Bill Johnson," a kind of political Robin Hood, who had conceived the idea of conferring on Canada the boon of freedom. The story of his devoted and daring daughter "Kate," who rowed him from hiding place to hiding place, and kept him supplied with food,

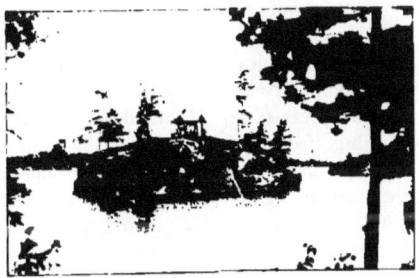

Oven Island, near Alexandria Bay.

gives a touch of the charm of legend and adventure to those rocky mazes.

The passage through the islands extends several hours. The steamer courses between Howe and Wolfe Islands, past Grindstone Island, stopping first at Clayton (New York), on the American mainland. It is a favorite summer resort, renowed for the splendid fishing in the vicinity, where black bass, pickerel and maskinongé abound. All lines of steamers stop at Clayton. It is connected with Niagara Falls, Albany, New York and Utica by railroad. The trip from New York and Utica can be made in thirteen and three hours, respectively, without any changing.

The scenery of the Thousand Islands, the advantages for boating, fishing and camping, and the purity of the climate, contribute towards making the region the most unique of Canada's pleasure grounds. Almost directly opposite Clayton, on the Canadian shore, is Gananoque, situated in the heart of the Thousand Islands. It is one of the best points from which to make the journey through this scenic paradise. Gananoque also boasts of a first-class hostelry, recently built, and called the "Gananoque Inn," and which is one of the finest hotels on the St. Lawrence River. The commodious passenger steamers running on the Thousand Islands route call several times daily. Tourists can stop over and spend a few days at this point with much profit, and the fishing in the locality is within a stone's throw of the hotel.

Office, Gananoque Inn.

Gananoque.

Within five minutes' walk from the Inn are the St. Lawrence Golf grounds, on a most picturesque position. A bowling-alley and billiard-tables, in connection with the hotel, provide amusement for rainy days.

The steamer for Montreal leaves Gananoque at 6.00 in the morning, from June 14th to July 9th, and daily from July 9th to September 3rd, for a trip through the Thousand Islands, and passengers in the sleeping cars arriving at this point by the Grand Trunk Railway from the west are permitted to remain in the car until a few minutes before the departure of the steamer.

Stave Island, in close contiguity to Gananoque, has been chosen several times as the camping ground of the American Canoe Association, and was selected for the 1898 meet. This locality

Stave Island. was decided upon owing to the freedom from swift currents, its health-giving pine woods and forests, and its suitable shores and bathing beaches. It is an unequalled spot for camps, boating and canoeing.

Leaving the Thousand Islands, we pass Morristown and Ogdensburg, while on the opposite shore are Brockville and Prescott, where connections are made for Ottawa, Montreal and the east and south.

The Gananoque Inn

From Clayton the steamer courses along the American channel of the river, past Round Island. This island (one mile by one thousand four hundred feet) is one of the finest gems in the entire

Round Island. Ariadne's Crown of Isles. Its many pretty cottages, beautiful grounds, luxuriant foliage, substantial docks and splendid water front, make it a most attractive spot for tourists. Round Island possesses a superb hotel, the Frontenac. It is a truly luxurious summer hotel, lighted by electricity, and with the most modern appointments. It is surrounded by beautiful lawns, is amply supplied with pleasure boats and yachts, has golf links and a bicycle path three miles around the island, and is, in one word, an ideal summer home.

A few miles farther on, in the very heart of the archipelago, the steamer passes Thousand Island Park, on Wellesley Island, an extensive summer resort laid out in small parks and avenues, and occupied by five to six hundred beautiful cottages. Originally established as a denominational park, it is now conducted by business men as a strictly undenominational resort, where, as at Chautauqua, the best speakers of all denominations are heard, and summer schools and university extension lectures are available at moderate charges. A fine and large hotel, "The Columbian," has been erected in this park, in the form of a Greek cross, thereby avoiding inside or badly ventilated rooms. The hotel is lighted by electricity, has a new water supply system, and is under able management.

The facilities for boating, fishing, driving or horseback riding are unsurpassed. Concerts and other entertainments fill up the week-day evenings for those who desire them.

There is much that appeals to the visitor's sense of the picturesque at this park.

The beautiful avenue along its water front gives far-reaching views of the flowing river upon one hand, and leafy vistas along the side avenues which lead into the heart of the park domain.

The run of the steamer from Thousand Island Park to Alexandria Bay is superb in the characteristic island scenery. Hundreds of islands lie across the steamer's tortuous and zig-zag course, all differing in size, coast and coloring, and forming an intricacy of channels through which only the experienced pilot could guide the way. Now we are entering a narrow pass between cliff-like banks covered with moss and trailing creepers, then we open into a lake-like expansion, then again among winding courses through clustering islands and around rocky points. We are here in the home of the canoe, of which hundreds are seen dotted over the surface of the water. Both sailing and paddling canoes are much in use and help to enliven the scene. Steam launches are in great vogue among the richer class, and sailing yachts and skiffs complete the pleasure craft in these waters.

Alexandria Bay.

We now emerge from the labyrinth into Alexandria Bay, the "Saratoga of the St. Lawrence," undoubtedly the central attraction of the whole summer life of the Thousand Islands. It is one of the

Stave Island, site of the A. C. A. Camp Meeting, 1898.

most popular as well as one of the most fashionable watering places in America, and numbers among its frequenters some of the wealthiest and best known men of the United States. The place boasts of several good hotels, besides numerous cottages of beautiful design. The adjacent islands are dotted with cottages in all sorts of pic-

Brockville.

turesque surroundings, some showing from among the trees perched on rocky bluffs, others snugly placed on low-lying islands and nestling in their beautiful coves. Thousands of people from all parts of the world visit this place annually, attracted hither by the fame of its natural beauty, wholesome atmosphere, pleasant society and excellent fishing. This Mecca of the pastime seekers of all America is built upon a massive pile of rocks, and has an excellent view of the Thousand Islands scenery. In the vicinity is a position whence a hundred isles can be seen at one view. Visitors to the Thousand Islands who wish to take the trip through the Bay of Quinte can do so by taking any of the Richelieu Company's steamers, on their trip up the river.

About opposite Alexandria Bay, on Wellesley Island, is the Presbyterian resort, Westminster Park. The portion of the island included in the park grounds consists of two hund. acres of ground, in formation an irregular neck of upland, rising to a mean elevation above the water of about forty feet, with rounded heights lifted to extremes of one hundred and fifty feet. From these summits, which are reached by easy s'opes, either in carriages or on foot, the whole group of the Thousand Islands, extending along the river for a distance of twenty miles, are brought into full view. The Westminster Park ferry connects with all steamers arriving at and departing from Alexandria Bay.

Westminster Park Hotel is most desirably situated on Westminster Park, directly opposite the village of Alexandria Bay, in close proximity to the best fishing grounds on the St. Lawrence River.

Leaving Alexandria Bay, the steamer runs down the widening channel among the outskirting islands, some decked with pine and firs, and some but arid granite rocks, until it passes the "Three Sisters," the final pickets of the archipelago, and leaves the Manatoana, the Garden of the Great Spirit, as the Indians named the Thousand Islands, finally behind.

Scarcely have we emerged from the still lingering images of the beautiful island scenery, when come in view the spires and roofs of the picturesque town of Brockville. This town, named after General
Brockville. Brock, the hero of Queenston Heights, 1812, is built on an elevation which ascends by successive ridges from the St. Lawrence. It is on the main line of the Grand Trunk Railway, and a branch of the Canadian Pacific Railway runs from it to Ottawa. It has connection by ferry with the Rome, Watertown and Ogdens-

Elevator of the Prescott Elevator Co

burg Railway. Its population is about nine thousand, and it is a progressive business centre.

Prescott. Prescott, named after General Prescott, a town of some four thousand inhabitants, just about opposite the American city of Ogdensburg, is the next port of call. Among its noteworthy places of interest are Fort Wellington, named after the Iron Duke, the Tomb of Barbara Heck, one of the founders of Methodism in America, at the little blue church on the river bank, and the famous Windmill, with its narrow loopholes peeping from its side. This is the windmill that figured in the insurrection of 1837 as the stronghold of the "Patriots" under the unhappy Van Schultze. These desperate men were forced to surrender, after several days' defence, and Van Schultze and nine others were executed at Fort Henry. The Government have since converted the Windmill into a splendid lighthouse.

Point Airy State Asylum (opposite Prescott).

Prescott has several large commercial houses, amongst others the J. P. Wiser Manufacturing Company's extensive distillery. Daniel's Hotel is a favorite resort for travellers.

Prescott is an important point in the water route of grain from the West seeking export *via* Montreal and the American Atlantic ports. In order to handle the grain taking this route, a fine elevator was built here, in the year 1895, for the Prescott Elevator Company, Limited. The storage capacity of this mammoth building is some 1,000,000 bushels. It is 72 feet wide by 280 long, and is built out into the river on pile foundations, surmounted by concrete piers and masonry. The depth of the water at the front of the building is 20 feet, and at the sides, where barges are loaded, 14 feet. During the 1898 season this elevator handled some 6,000,000 bushels of grain.

The Richelieu & Ontario Navigation Co.

The Prescott Elevator Company also operate a line of barges between Prescott and Montreal for the purpose of transhipping grain to Montreal en route for export.

Leaving this historic ground, the steamer courses serenely on her way, and now bearing to the right discloses the imposing group of buildings of the Point Airy New York State Asylum. We give on page 48 an illustration of central administration building. Perched upon the banks which overhang the river, their situation is magnificent. A little further on, to the left, is Chimney Island, which during the French régime was strongly fortified. The calm stretch of the river, varied here and there by a few islands, would scarcely prepare one for the boisterous scenes ahead. But soon after the last glimpse of Prescott fades in the distance, we pass through the first of the troubled waters of the St. Lawrence, the Gallops. These are only a foretaste of what is to follow, for as the spires and roof tops of the town of Morrisburg are seen through the trees, we find ourselves, on rounding an intervening point, in full view of the Rapids du Plat, as they swirl their dark green waters among a group of wooded islands and beneath the shadows of their overhanging trees.

After shooting the du Plat, the steamer glides with steadily increasing motion past a picturesque point named Woodlands and in among bolder shores, on the north side of Croyles Island, into sight of the turbulent waters of the Long Sault, with its snow-crested billows of raging water. This, the first one of the really remarkable rapids of the St. Lawrence, extends some nine miles down stream to Cornwall, divided into two main channels by numerous beautifully wooded islands. The "shooting of

Long Sault Rapids.

Old Windmill, near Prescott.
(Held by Patriot Rebels in 1837.)

the rapids," as the descent by boat is called, is a most exciting experience. Before us is a seething mass of churning waters, rushing with headlong speed down a declivity which stretches ahead, apparently without termination, as far as the eye can reach. Each moment we feel ourselves and our great vessel being further drawn into the Charybdis jaws of the mighty current among its angry darkling eddies, past jutting headlands, close to insidious rocks ; while the roar of the surges, the foaming spray that dashes over the vessel, intensifies the excitement caused by her swift downward and undulating movement. With her steam almost completely shut off, she dashes in among the waves that seem to advance to meet her up the hill, and is carried along, by sheer force of the current, at a speed of twenty miles an hour, guided alone by the extra-manned helm, past what seem to be dangerous places, amid the ocean roar and tumult of the lashing surf. Navigation of the Long Sault requires exceptional nerve and precision in piloting, as well as extra power to control the helm ; hence, in "shooting the rapids," the rudder is provided with a tiller (besides the regular apparatus), and this is manned, while four men are kept at the wheel to ensure safe steering ; and, as a result of such precautions, fatal accidents are unknown.

The first passage of the Long Sault by steamer was made about 1840, under the pilotage of the celebrated Indian Terorhiahere. The channel followed was that which has until recently been considered the only safe one, namely, the southern, on the American side of the dividing islands. But examinations have been made in these later days, and the northern channel proven quite navigable, so that it has become as much the highway of steamboat traffic as the southern.

To the right is the picturesque Indian village of St. Regis, with its little cluster of houses and the glittering roof of its church standing conspicuously among them. The church, or rather its bell, is connected with an historical incident of savage Indian revenge, in the early days. On its passage from France, the bell was captured by an English cruiser, taken to Salem, Mass., and sold to the church at Deerfield, of the same state. The St. Regis Indians, hearing of the capture and the destination of their bell, proceeded stealthily to Deerfield, attacked the town, massacred forty-seven of the inhabitants, and brought one hundred and twelve captives back with them, along with the bell, which now hangs in the St. Regis church.

The Richelieu & Ontario Navigation Co. 51

Cornwall. Nearly opposite this pretty Indian village, on the left, is the thriving town of Cornwall, with its extensive woollen and cotton mills. The completion of the Cornwall Canal, some twelve miles long, with seven locks, offers a safe passage to small craft on the eastern journey, and is the only course possible for all craft bound westward. We are now near the line which divides Canada from the United States, as well as the line separating Eastern Ontario from Quebec. The bed of the St. Lawrence expands near Cornwall, forming the beautiful Lake St. Francis. The shores on either side present a pleasing prospect, diversified with woods and farms. "But," says a well-known writer, "the chief glory of a sail down Lake St. Francis, is the distant mountain range, blue against the horizon, filling up the lack which the eye has vaguely felt in the flat, unbroken horizon which bounds the greater part of Ontario. It is the Châteauguay range—a spur of the Adirondacks—sometimes drawing nearer, sometimes receding into cloud-like indistinctness." At the entrance to the lake we pass Stanley Island. This is a desirable summer resort,

Algonquin Hotel, Stanley Island.

within fifty miles of Montreal, and in the fall is a very central spot for hunting, etc. The Algonquin Hotel, situated on the island, is well fitted up, and, with pleasant surroundings, claims a good share of popularity. At the lower end of the lake we draw up by the long wooden pier of Coteau-du-Lac, whose straggling row of **Coteau.** little French houses, looking still smaller in contrast with the great stone church and gleaming spire, gives evidence that we are now in French Canada. A charming scene does this old Coteau make as seen at sunset on the return trip, when Lake St. Francis, still as a mirror, reflects the rich crimsons and purples of the descending sun; while the old brown timbers of the pier, and the equally old and brown French Canadian houses, with the rather Dutch-looking boats moored by the pier, compose a picture to which only a Turner could do justice.

Across from Coteau, on the southern side, is the distant town of Valleyfield, with its huge cotton mill, at the upper end of the Beauharnois Canal.

After leaving Coteau Landing, the steamer passes under the magnificent iron bridge of the Canada Atlantic Railway, one of the greatest engineering masterpieces that adorn the St. Lawrence. It is about one mile and a half long. Shortly below this bridge the

Indian Village of Caughnawaga, opposite Lachine.

Coteau Rapids are entered. This is a very beautiful stretch of rapids about two miles in length, and frequently having an exceedingly swift current. It was among them that the detachment of men, sent to Montreal during General Amherst's expedition (1759), were lost.

About seven miles further down, we sweep past a small island whose thickly foliaged trees almost dip at the margin into the hurrying stream, round a sharp curve into the Cedar Rapids. This is a very turbulent stretch of water, and its passage is most exciting. At times the steamer seems to be settling as to sink, but she swiftly glides from threatening danger, from ominous rock to rock, until she emerges from the rapids.

But scarcely has she left the Cedar when she enters what, on approach, bodes to be the most perilous of all — the Split Rock Rapids — sentineled by huge boulders guarding the entry. One cannot help a shudder of fear as the ship approaches this threatening rock, but the skilful hand of the helmsman, at the opportune moment, deftly turns the boat aside, and it passes away unscathed.

The Cascades, the last of this series of rapids, is conspicuous by its white-crested waves, which mount tumultuously from the dark green waters in such a choppy, angry way, that they make the vessel lurch and toss as though at sea. This group of four rapids, following one another in close succession, have a descent of eighty-two and one-half feet, and extend, in all, about eleven miles.

Below the Cascades, the river expands into Lake St. Louis. Almost at its head, where the Cascades' seething waters soften into calm, the Ottawa River discharges one of its branches into the broad St. Lawrence, and the dark waters of the northern stream glide into the calm deep bottom of the great river, to find a purer home and greater glory in the resplendent beauty of the lake. On a high spot, along the south shore of this beautiful St. Louis Lake, is a cross reared, like the serpent in the wilderness, for men to look unto in time of peril and distress—symbols not only of human weakness and human need, but of divine support by faith in Him who, raised upon the cross, was typified by the brazen symbol of the Arabian wilds. The scenery is very fine along this lake. Calm and shadowy, the Châteauguay hills rear their lofty heads behind the trees, lower down the dim outline of Mount Royal can be seen, while further on, the cloudy tops of Belœil, St. Johns and Shefford loom against the

Canadian Pacific Railway Bridge, Lachine.

sky. From the point of confluence of the Ottawa and St. Lawrence, the shore, on our left as we go down, is the Island of Montreal. Along its margin can be seen the cottages of campers from Montreal, who come here in large numbers to spend the summer months. It is a most pleasant place of resort, both on account of its convenient proximity to the city and on account of its engaging scenery and wholesome surroundings. There are several yacht and boating club houses here and there ; amongst others, the Royal St. Lawrence Yacht Club, a little above the head of Dorval Island, which has for the last three years held the trophy of the Seawanhaka Yacht Club for small yachts.

After issuing from the lake, we come to the town of Lachine, nine miles from Montreal. This place is associated with the name of La Salle, who, about the year 1670, obtained a grant of land from the Seminary of Montreal, and here formed a settlement, giving to it the name of Lachine. It was La Salle who, during his wanderings in the land of the Illinois, first pitched upon Chicago as a trading post.

Lachine.

At this village the famous Lachine Canal commences, having been built to overcome the descent of the river in the Lachine Rapids. Even as we pass along, we can see the enclosed waters of the canal bearing upon their bosom the huge form of some up-going steamer. It is to this little village of Lachine that people come from Montreal by train to shoot the rapids. A most exciting method is to shoot the rapids in a skiff, under the skilful guidance of the Indians. It is apparently, at first sight, impossible for so small a boat to live in so wild a current of waters, but the Indians are so thoroughly acquainted with the shoals and dangerous places, as well as with the frantic humors of the fierce current, that the feat is sometimes risked by those seeking excitement.

Across from Lachine is the Indian village, Caughnawaga, on the south bank of the river. Its name, meaning "praying Indian," is very appropriately attached to the inhabitants, who are devoted adherents of the Roman Catholic faith, and annually, in June, join in the celebration of the Fête-Dieu, accoutred in their tribal paint and ornaments.

After passing this village, we come to the magnificent iron bridge of the Canadian Pacific Railway. It is a beautiful structure, built on the cantilever principle, much resembling the International Railway Bridge at Niagara.

The Richelieu & Ontario Navigation Co. 55

Passing under the bridge, the steamer glides into the mid-stream that moves with the calm majesty of irresistible power and speed, indicative of the coming rapids, which appear full in view as we sweep around an intercepting curve. And now we are before the fiercest, most celebrated, most difficult

Lachine Rapids.

A Richelieu Steamer entering the Lachine Rapids.

of navigation, as well as the last of the great St. Lawrence rapids—the Lachine. A universal stillness reigns among the passengers on deck, and their hearts throb with a dubious expectation as they look forward to the glittering sheet of foaming breakers ahead, with their two little green islets, dashing through the spray. Human speech can find no tongue in such a scene, but awe and the overpowering sense of the mighty forces in raging activity around, inspires the thrilling stillness of a mingled fear and pleasure in every soul—fear at the awful possibility of some miscarriage in our descent, pleasure in the triumphant exhibition of the "flash and cloud of the cascade, of the earthquake and foam-fire of the cataract," combined with the howling multitude of waters and the vast sweep and surging of the ocean wave. In we plunge among the breakers, and the headlong current bears us towards the shelving and insidious rocks, sometimes hidden, sometimes disclosed to view, with the dark suggestion of others couched unseen beneath the water. Deftly we pass them by, within a few yards of their treacherous edges, through foam, through mountain billows, with our bows sometimes apparently submerged, through hurrying eddy and swirling whirlpool, through clouds of spray ascending from the churning abyss crowned with the irridescence of a hundred rainbows, and amid the thunderous voices of the surging deeps. A moment more, we have completed the descent and ride in tranquility the placid bosom of the river beneath, with a sense of relief born of the contemplated danger past. Had we but deviated to right or left by so much as a few yards, or cast our length athwart the stream, we had been hurled by the angry current upon the rocks, to utter wreck, or instantly capsized, submerged and rolled amid a raging wilderness of waves. But the cool hand and clear eye of the pilot is equal to the perilous work, and it is a notable fact that no accident of any consequence has ever happened nor has a single life been lost in the course of many years of steamboat navigation on these wonderful rapids.

Most people prefer the wildness and grandeur of the Long Sault to the path of the Lachine Rapids, and no tourist should miss the Long Sault, as without this experience running the rapids of the St. Lawrence is incomplete.

Passing by the beautifully wooded shores of Nuns' Island, we come before the famous Victoria Jubilee Bridge — a magnificent structure of modern engineering achievement, and which was built to replace the Victoria Tubular Bridge, at one time the wonder

of the continent and one of the great engineering feats of the age.
The new bridge ranks, from an engineering standpoint, with the
foremost structures of the present age. The bridge contains double
tracks and a carriage-way and foot-walks on both sides, and each
span has been so erected that it will carry not only a train on each
track, moving in opposite directions, but going at the rate of 45
miles an hour, with a total weight of 4,000 lbs. to the lineal foot; an
electric train going at the rate of 25 miles an hour, as well as drive-
ways and foot-walks crowded with passengers and vehicles. It con-

Victoria Jubilee Bridge, G. T. R., Montreal.

meets Montreal with the south shore of the St. Lawrence by the Grand
Trunk Railway, and thus, with the Canadian Pacific Railway Bridge
above, provides the alternative route by rail across the river. It was
originally built of iron on the tubular principle. There are twenty-
four piers of solid masonry, extending in all some two miles. It
gives the impression of neatness and beauty. It is a grand sight to
stand upon this bridge, looking forth from one of the spans, and
watch the shipping passing underneath upon the bosom of the
curling waters, to see the hurrying streams gather in mounds before
each pier, then glide away on either side in angry eddy and in wave ;
to look along the row of massive piers converging in the distance,
with the great iron trusses upon their shoulders, reaching into
Montreal.

Sweeping beneath the great bridge, we come in full view of the city of Montreal, with its teeming harbor, with its beautiful public buildings of massive stone; its churches, its cathedrals, with gleaming pinnacles and domes and cupolas; its famous parks; its learning, its colleges; and, most of all, with its royal mountain, lifting its imperial head above the rush and din of commerce, like an altar, open to great and small, to rich and poor, to come to, offering up their sacrifice of adoration for so much beauty and grandeur freely given them, both from the hand of man and from the hand of nature. As we move through the crowded harbor, we pass, here and there,

Immigrants' Memorial Stone.

the huge forms of ocean vessels at their moorings. Away ahead we catch a glimpse of the towers of Notre-Dame and the massive dome of St James rising above the other structures, giving a distant foretaste, in their sunset glory, of the myriad beauties which lie wrapt in the hidden bosom of the splendid city. We come to port near St. Helen's Island, once a military stronghold, but now transformed into a magnificent park; the steamer first stopping at Commissioners' wharf, to transfer its passengers to the Quebec steamer, and then continuing to the canal basin.

As tourists generally prefer to visit Montreal on their way home, we will reserve for the return trip a description of the interesting points of the city, and sail on down the St. Lawrence towards Quebec and the Saguenay.

The journey down the St. Lawrence, from Montreal to Quebec, in one of the palatial steamers that ply on this route, is as pleasant a trip as could be taken anywhere in America. Leaving Montreal in the evening, we first pass Longueuil, a small village on the south bank, and the summer residence of many Montrealers. Longueuil

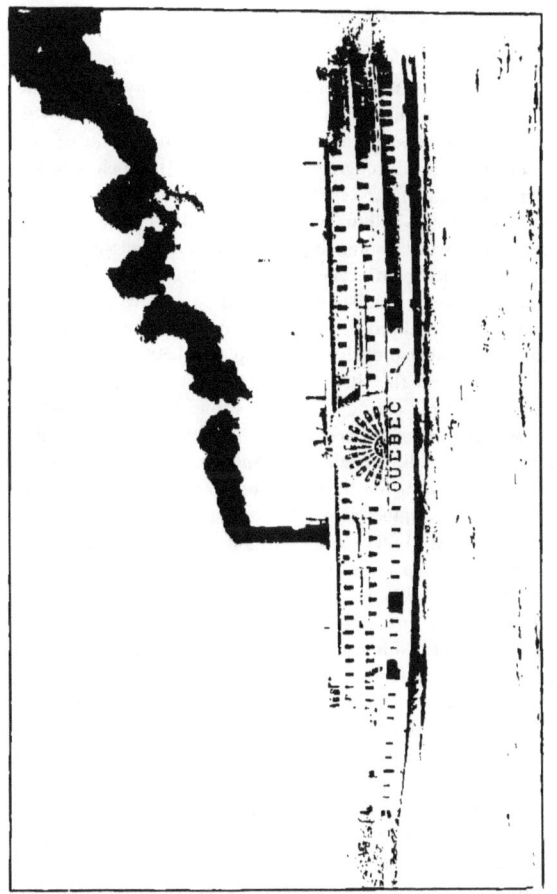

The R. & O. Co.'s Steamer "Quebec."

is memorable in history for the repulse of General Carleton, in 1775, by the Americans. A little down on the north shore is Longue Pointe. At a distance of nine miles from Montreal, we see Pointeaux Trembles, founded in 1674. Here is one of the old French churches, built in 1709. Just below it are the Islands of Boucherville. These islands are mostly low and flat, with very shallow water among them, and a thick growth of reeds and weeds, affording excellent duck shooting and pike fishing, but wanting in scenery from their extreme flatness. Here it is that the ice grounds on the break up of winter, occasionally causing an inundation. At a distance of fifteen miles is Varennes, one of the most prettily situated places between Montreal and Quebec. I lies with the St. Lawrence in front and the Richelieu in its rear Mineral springs of great value are situated here. At a distance of forty miles is Berthier, on the north shore, opposite to the entrance of the Richelieu, and to numerous islands similar to those of Boucherville ; still five miles farther down, at the junction of the Richelieu, is Sorel, lately raised to the dignity of a city. Sorel was once called William Henry, after William IV, who, when in the navy, and lying off Quebec, visited this place, coming up in his vessel to Lake St. Peter, whence he took a small boat upwards. It stands on the site of the fort built by de Tracy in 1665, and was for many years the summer residence of successive governors of Canada. There is splendid snipe shooting in this neighborhood in October, and very good fishing all through the year, among the numerous islands which here stud the surface of the river. About five miles further down, the river expands into a vast sheet of water, about twenty-five miles long and nine miles broad, which is known as Lake St. Peter. This lake is, for the most part, quite shallow, except in the channel, which has been dredged so as to enable the largest ocean steamers to pass up and down. In passing through this lake the traveller is sure to see several rafts on their way downwards. The songs of the raftsmen were once a delightful melody on these waters, but the towing system has done away with much of the old romance of the river.

Passing the mouth of the St. Francis, which flows in from the Eastern Townships, near which is a settlement of the Abenaquis Indians, we arrive at the city of Three Rivers, situated on the north shore of the St. Lawrence, at the mouth of the St. Maurice River, which here separates into three channels, whence the name of the

View of the City of Quebec from Lévis.

city is derived, and lying about midway between Quebec and Montreal, being about ninety miles from either of the cities. This is a most interesting place in many respects. Benjamin Sulte, the French Canadian poet and historian, has worked its mines of historical lore to noble uses, and given it a fame greater than its lumber and iron industries could ever achieve. The French began the smelting of iron here as early as 1737. Three Rivers is the see of a Roman Catholic bishopric.

The cathedral is a stately edifice, and the neighborhood is rich in associations to any one who cares to explore hem.

Opposite Three Rivers is Doucet's Landing, the terminus of the Athabaska and Three Rivers branch of the Grand Trunk Railway, thus keeping this section easy of access from the south, as the railway on the north shore does on the other side. Here we may be said to be at the head of tide water, the home of the tommy-cod fishery. Continuing the journey, we pass Batiscan, called after a famous Indian chief known to the first settlers ; then Ste. Anne and the Jacques-Cartier River, after which the land on the river banks begins to rise, presenting a more bold and picturesque appearance as we near Quebec. Ste. Augustine and St. Antoine, two pretty villages, are soon passed, and the mouth of the Chaudière is the next object of interest. Here, some twelve or more miles from Quebec, in the seclusion of the woods, are the falls of the Chaudière, a river which, flowing through the auriferous district of the Eastern Townships, and abounding, through its course of one hundred miles, in rapids, precipitates itself downward over a hundred feet into a rocky and chaotic basin, where, during the spring floods, the roaring of the waters and the fantastic cliffs and hedges on either side combine to make a deep impression on the mind.

Continuing our way, we come to Pointe Lévis, nearly opposite Quebec, on the south-western shore. Before us is the grand gateway of the St. Lawrence, the famous Citadel of Quebec, with its majestic memories of mystery, adventure, victory and defeat — the battle-ground where Wolfe won for England, and the Celto-Britannic race, the illimitable Dominion of the North and West.

From these high cliffs, and from under these grey old walls, the first pioneers of what is now the granary of the world, went forth into the unknown wilderness. From this antique city, also, departed the first missionaries, carrying the message of the cross to distant tribes and nations. But that which must forever give Quebec chief claim to the attention of the traveller is its historical battlefield

Quebec. which has seen the fiercest and most momentous battles in the early history of North America, and on which both France and England's generals perished in the final struggle for the possession of Canada. It is impossible to stand here and reflect on the momentous consequences of Wolfe's victory without feeling the influence of the spirit of the scene. But philosophic melancholy in these days gives way at Quebec to more joyful influences, for it is one of the most delightful places, socially, to be found anywhere in the world. Whether it be summer or winter, the people of the Ancient Capital take full enjoyment out of life, and strive to make the stranger feel at home. Founded by Samuel de Champlain, A. D. 1608, nearly three centuries have given the fortress city a history rich in material for the philosopher, the poet and the romancer. Among the records, associations and scenes thus brought together, the traveller, if so inclined, may find endless fields for research, acquaintanceship or observation. He will find the pretty souvenir book, "Illustrated Quebec," which he can buy for one dollar, a charming guide and memento of his visit.

> To all old friends, to those who dwell,
> Secure, in yonder Citadel
> To old Quebec, whose glorious fame
> Few cities of to-day may claim;
> Quebec past, present and to be,
> Greeting; our pen shall tell of thee.

Quaint, curious old Quebec, whose winding streets and frowning battlements are pervaded with the atmosphere of departed centuries, here is the spot where the refined luxury of the Old World first touched the barbaric wilderness of the New; here is the cradle of Canada. Quebec seems to have been specially formed by Nature for the important part assigned to her in the drama of this continent, for, from her commanding eminence, she holds the position of guardian and sentry of Canada. In reviewing the history of Quebec, we meet the interesting figure of that intrepid explorer, Jacques Cartier. In 1535 Jacques Cartier sailed from France, under a commission from Francis I, in the hope of discovering a new highway to the Indies, and also of adding to the possessions of his native land. Sailing up the magnificent river, he gave to it the name of St. Lawrence, and, on the 14th of September, he reached the mouth of a little tributary, which he called Ste. Croix. Here he cast anchor. The natives of the village of Stadacona, headed by their chief, Donnacona, paddled out in their birch-bark canoes to meet the strangers, having been attracted by the novelty of their wondrous vessels.

The meeting of Jacques Cartier and the chiefs appears to have been friendly, for he willingly conducted the explorers to the summit of the rock, and to the little village that nestled beneath. What a wondrous picture was spread out before him from this noble height. Clothed in the primeval grandeur of Nature, enriched with the glory of autumnal tints, no prospect could be more enchanting, no wealth more unbounded, than that which was enfolded in the bosom of these mighty solitudes. Jacques Cartier had yet to learn that there was another side to this rosy picture, for, with the fading of the leaves, the first signs of winter approached. Beautiful, indeed, are the winters of Canada; but we are prepared for them—Cartier was not. Untold were the sufferings of these explorers during the five months that they were bound in the grip of ice and snow. With the return of spring, Jacques Cartier sailed again for France, but nothing came of his voyage. The time had not yet come, and nearly a century was to elapse before the founder of New France appeared. In 1608 Samuel de Champlain planted the white flag of France upon the heights of Quebec. Champlain was a man of undaunted courage, a soldier, sailor, statesman, and possessing the heart and soul of a hero. No man was ever more fitted to found, develope and rule an empire than he. And it is to his untiring efforts and genius that we are indebted for the Canada of to-day.

But let us wend our way through the winding streets, until we gain the summit of the frowning rocks, where we can take in a view

City Hall, Quebec.

none the less beautiful than that which met the gaze of Champlain or Jacques Cartier. From Dufferin Terrace, or from the Citadel, still higher, the picture spread out beneath our feet can nowhere be duplicated. Here the lily banner of the Bourbons and the time-worn flag of England have been unfurled in token of supremacy. All the memory-haunted scenes of a glorious past sweep before our gaze. Yonder is the spot where the noblest sons of France and England fought for the empire of this land, in the memorable battle of the Plains of Abraham. No pen is needed to tell the glory of their death. Behind Dufferin Terrace, in the Governor's Garden, the granite column tells their story, by its simple inscription : " In memory of Wolfe and Montcalm." Vanquisher and vanquished lie silent in the tomb, but their names are linked together in an indissoluble wreath of glory. Nestled together below us are the antique gables, the peculiar roofs, the quaint spires and the historic walls that take us back into the last century, and side by side with them,

Grand Battery, Quebec.

increasing their interest, are the grand modern structures of the present.

With a copy of "Illustrated Quebec" in hand, we commence a leisurely survey of the picture before us. Every stone in the walls of Quebec has a history, and every spot of ground is rendered sacred by the events of the past.

Behind us rise the grey walls of the ancient citadel, and immediately under us is the city, with its strange confusion of buildings, all cast, as it were, at random upon the declivities of a mountain, and tumbling down in wild confusion to the shores of the great river below. We do not propose going into all the details of the peculiar historical attractions of Quebec ; we will take a rapid glance at the scene before us.

Looking away beyond the churches and monuments, the ramparts and gates, we behold a picture that no pencil could delineate and no poet could describe. Over the heights of Lévis, and above its frowning fortifications, rises the summer sun ; his beams gild the spires of a hundred historic buildings, each with a story that might be the basis of a real romance. Still looking to the right, the Isle of Orleans divides the waters of the St. Lawrence, and looks up to the Citadel as a child to a protecting parent. Then across the stream—

> "Where yonder mountains, cracked
> And sundered by volcanic fire,
> Sings Moutmorency's cataract,—
> Fit chord for such a granite lyre."

Then the long, thin village of Beauport stretches its serpentine length along the shore and basks in the rays of the rising sun. Beyond the Beauport Flats arise the blue Laurentians, mound over mound, till they blend with a few fleecy clouds upon the distant horizon. From out the forest and fields glances the steeple of the Charlesbourg church — a hamlet with a history of its own. Behind this again appears the humble, but still more interesting, chapel of the Indian village of Lorette. Lorette, the home of the Huron, the last resting-place of that warrior tribe, as its braves disappear like snow before the sun of civilization. Of yore, the Huron of Lorette treated with Montcalm, and fired his arrows at the invader; to-day the old chief sits at his door and teaches the rising generation to shoot arrows at the copper and silver pieces which the traveler sets up to test their skill. Still turning west-
ward, we notice the sinuosities of the St.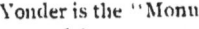
Charles, as it rolls through green meadows down to its confluence with the St. Lawrence.
Yonder is the "Monu-
ment of the
Brave," on

the Ste. Foye Road; beside it is a Martello tower; nearer still is the Wolfe shaft on the Plains—scenes once glorious and terrible in the days of immemorable conflict.

We will start our visit to the city with the Château Frontenac. The site of this beautiful hotel is that of the ancient Château St. Louis, for above two centuries the seat of the government of the province. The hall of the old fort, in the early days of the colony, was often the scene of ter.or and despair at the inroads of the Iroquois, who, having passed all the French outposts, threatened the fort itself, and massacred some friendly Indians within sight of its walls.

The Château Frontenac is a magnificent new fire-proof hotel, situated at the eastern end of Dufferin Terrace, commanding delightful views of the St. Lawrence as far as the eye can reach—down past the Isle of Orleans, across to Lévis and beyond, up stream to Sillery, and, to the left, the country along the beautiful valley of the St. Charles River. It has been planned with that strong sense of the fitness of things. In exterior it blends with its surroundings; it is part of the wondrous picturesqueness, while the interior is a monument to the skill of the architect, who has retained the maximum of comfort and beauty without sacrificing the outlook, which has been obtained by constructing the hotel in the shape of a horseshoe.

Martello Tower

The foundations of the original castle, dating 1620, can be seen still under Dufferin Terrace.

The Hotel Victoria is another of Quebec's hotels. Overlooking the valley of the St. Charles River, it is situated within one block of the Grand Battery, and commands a delightful view. Turkish, Russian, electric and swimming baths are connected with this hotel, whose range of prices are well in keeping with a modest purse, while the tourist's comfort is well looked after.

Dufferin Terrace was first laid out by the Earl of Durham, Governor-General of Canada in 1838. During the administration of the Marquis of Dufferin and Ava, however, it was improved and enlarged into the present promenade, and has since been known as Dufferin Terrace.

"Of all the historic monuments," writes Sir James LeMoine, "connecting modern Quebec with its eventful and historic past, none more deservedly hold a high place in the estimation of the antiquarian, the scholar and the curious stranger than the former

In Champlain Street, Lower Town, Quebec.

gates of the renowned fortress. These relics of a bygone age, with their massive proportions and grim mediæval architecture, no longer exist, however, to carry the mind back to the days which invest the oldest city in North America with its peculiar interest and attraction." But Quebec is still a fortress, and, through the efforts of Lord Dufferin, a scheme of restoration was carried out which preserves the ancient character of the city and facilitates the requirements of modern progress.

A stroll around the ramparts, and an inspection of the picturesque and substantial archways gives the visitor a good idea of the military strength of the city. In the midst of these standing evidences of defiance or defence, we may trace the dominant influence of a greater power in the embodiment of its religious institutions, still breathing the monastic spirit of the seventeenth century. Crowning the cliffs stands the University of Laval, the chief seat of French culture in the Dominion. In its foundations may be traced the intellectual development of the country. To the visitor the university possesses a peculiar charm, and many a priceless relic and work of art may be found within its walls. It has been called after the famous bishop, Mgr. de Laval de Montmorenci, who endowed it liberally, as did all his successors. Apart from the boarding house—for medical and law students—and the special buildings for the medical classes, the main body of the university consists of an immense six-story edifice about two hundred and fifty feet in length and seventy in depth. It looks down from the high rock—two hundred feet above the river—upon the most magnificent scene that Nature, combined with human invention, can present in America. Its triple towers and cross-crowned cupola seem to rise in the very heavens. Imposing as the edifice is from the outside, it is a treasure house within. Its lecture halls, its professors' rooms, its classes in chemistry, physics and mechanical science—filled with specimens of every modern invention or appliance, would suffice to keep a stranger hours in pleasant investigation. Its vast library, one of the most extensive and rare in Canada, is a treasure in itself. Its museum certainly surpasses anything of the class in the country. Among the celebrated masters represented in the gallery of Laval may be mentioned Salvator Rosa, Teniers, Romenelli, Joseph Vernet, Paget and Perocci Poussin.

On the cliff, near the entrance, may be pointed out the spot where the gallant General Montgomery fell, at the head of the storming party, December 31, 1775.

Another fine edifice that claims our attention is the Basilica, near the old Market Square. It is built on the site of the ancient church of Notre-Dame-de-la-Recouvrance, erected in 1633, by Samuel de Champlain, to commemorate the restoration of the colony by Britain. Within this ancient church were interred the remains of Laval—perhaps the most historic figure in the annals of New France—Frontenac, and many other of her worthies.

Notre-Dame-des-Victoires.

The Basilica contains, amongst other valuable paintings, the Christ of the Cathedral, by Van Dyke, and the Ecstasy of St. Paul, by Carlo Maratti. Some of the pictures were brought to Canada from France during the Revolution. The square opposite, where the new City Hall has been erected, is the site of the old Jesuit College, the last trace of which was removed a few years ago. There is interest even in the site of this old building, for it was the oldest college in America, dating from the year 1635. Within its walls the martyrs Lalemant, Brebeuf and Vipond taught, and Père Marquette drew his plans that led to the establishment of Christianity on the banks of the Mississippi. Adjoining the Basilica is the Archbishop's Palace, the residence of his Grace Archbishop Bégin.

The next building that claims our attention is the Ursuline Convent, on Garden street. The convent is beautifully situated in a garden of seven acres extent, and owes its origin to the religious zeal of Mme de la Peltrie and Mère Marie de l'Incarnation, two remarkable women, whose devotion has formed themes for poets and historians. The date of the earliest foundation was 1641, and of the present 1686. There is a small picture preserved here which portrays a touching tradition of the early days of Canada. Montcalm, who fell so gloriously in the battle contending with Wolfe for supremacy on the Heights of Abraham, is buried in the chapel. Lord Aylmer, governor-general of Canada in 1831, caused a simple marble tablet to be placed above the tomb, bearing this inscription:

HONNEUR
À
MONTCALM
LE DESTIN EN LUI DÉROBANT LA VICTOIRE
L'A RÉCOMPENSÉ PAR UNE MORT GLORIEUSE

Montcalm's tomb is said to have been formed by the bursting of a shell during the siege of the city.

The Hôtel-Dieu, or Hospital of the Precious Blood, was founded in 1639, by a neice of Cardinal Richelieu. During the seventeenth century it played an important part in the religious life of the French colony. Attached to the convent is the chapel which contains the bones of Father Lalemant and the skull of Father Jean de Brebeuf. An interesting episode in the history of Canada, during the last century, attaches to a relic in the possession of the Ladies of the Hôtel-Dieu. In 1742 a soldier of the Montreal garrison professed to be a sorcerer, and, in furtherance of his pretensions, had profaned sacred objects. He had taken a crucifix, and,

Monument to Wolfe and Montcalm, Quebec.

covering it with an inflammable substance, exposed it to the flames, at the same time reciting certain passages of Scripture. Public indignation was so great that he was arrested and sentenced to make public reparation in front of the parish church of Montreal. The Bishop of Quebec obtained the crucifix and presented it to the Ladies of the Hôtel-Dieu, where it is still piously preserved.

Hope Hill, Quebec.

A place that is especially attractive to visitors from the United States is number 42 St. Louis street. In it were deposited the remains of Brigadier General Montgomery, on the 31st of December, 1775.

The quaint old church of Notre-Dame-des-Victoires, erected in 1688, must also be visited, as it is associated with several warlike events: the memorable repulse of Sir William Phipps' attack on Quebec, on the 16th October, 1690, and the providential escape of the town from surrender to Sir Hovenden Walker's formidable fleet, wrecked on the 22nd August, 1711. During the siege of Quebec, in 1759, a portion of the church was destroyed by the batteries from Lévis.

On the north side of the Place d'Armes, coming off the Dufferin Terrace, is the Union building, erected in 1805, upon the site of a previous building occupied as a residence, in 1649, by Governor D'Ailleboust. This building has a very interesting history. Originally occupied by the famous Barons' Club, it was afterwards used as the Union and St. George's hotels, and as

government offices. It was under this roof that war was declared with the United States in 1812. It is owned by D. Morgan, one of the pioneer tailors, established over a century, who has enjoyed a long and successful reign.

Every turn that we take in Quebec brings us face to face with some memorial of the past, and most of its streets perpetuate the names of its worthies. Among the curious streets that every visitor is sure to see may be mentioned Sous-le-Cap and the site of the once famous Breakneck Stairs. Even that modern-looking building, the Post Office, has its history, for it is built on the site of an old legendary haunted house known as *Le Chien d'Or*. There, in the wall, we can see the curious old stone, with its inscription, and its golden dog gnawing its bone as of old, and in Mr. Kirby's novel, "The Golden Dog," we can learn still further of its history.

A very enjoyable tour may be made, commencing at the Dufferin Terrace, along St. Louis street. On the right is the Place d'Armes, a pretty square; a military parade ground in the days of the French

Provincial Parliament Buildings, Quebec.

régime. On the left is Kent House, the residence of the Duke of Kent while in Canada. It has not many attractions to offer to the tourist, but in its day it was regarded as a palace. In striking contrast is the Court House, on the opposite side of the street. But

Court House, Quebec.

contrasts are common in Quebec, for here the old and new meet together as they meet nowhere else on the continent. Close by is the Music Hall, and opposite is the little old-fashioned house once occupied as the headquarters of General Montcalm. Here he held his councils of war and prepared his plans for the defence of the city in 1759. Further on we pass the Esplanade, beside the city walls, used by the British troops as a parade-ground. From here we can see the Garrison Club, a very interesting place, and much appreciated by the officers. Immediately outside the gate, on the right, is the Skating Rink, and here we come in view of the handsome buildings of the Provincial Legislature, which overlook the historic Plains of Abraham.

Turning into those extensive fields that reach from St. Louis Road to the cliffs over Wolfe's Cove, and from the Citadel to Spencerwood, the residence of the Lieutenant-Governor, the tourist finds himself walking upon soil rendered sacred by the heroic memories of the

past. There, beneath the monument that tells a glorious story—
"Here Wolfe fell victorious,"—are the ashes of countless heroes.
On such a spot well might the lines of Campbell be repeated :

> " Few, few shall part where many meet,
> The snow shall be their winding-sheet,
> And every turf beneath your feet
> Shall be a soldier's sepulchre."

Beyond are the Martello towers, built in 1812 for the better defence of the city's fortifications. Below you, on the Ste. Foye Road—which is reached by the Belvedere Drive,—stands the Monument of the Brave. It has been erected to commemorate the heroism of the men who perished at the battle of Ste. Foye.

We must now leave Quebec and cross over on the ferryboat to Pointe Lévis, the opposite shore. This place is equally as interesting, in proportion to its size, as is Quebec itself. The finest possible view of the old city is to be had from the Lévis heights. Especially at night, when a thousand electric lights flash upon the scene, Quebec resembles a Venice, plus the frowning citadel and terraces of brilliancy rising one above the other.

It was from Lévis that the British cannon played upon Quebec in 1759. The fortifications to-day are of a superior class in every

Grande Allée and St. Louis Gate, Quebec.

sense. Immense sums have been spent upon the forts and batteries of the hilly town. From the heights a magnificent view of the Montmorency Falls can be had, and the drives around Lévis are as picturesque and attractive as those that lead from Quebec to the numerous points of interest that surround the place.

Before saying adieu to these scenes of heroism, to the crumbling relics of ancient Quebec, the tourist should join the pilgrim procession to that spot hallowed by the mystery of numerous miraculous cures, visited by hundreds of thousands of pilgrims annually—the Canadian Mecca—Ste. Anne-de-Beaupré. Let us leave Quebec by the Quebec, Montmorency and Charlevoix Railway, and, as we fly along, take a glance at the beauties of the surrounding country.

The sun flings a sheet of glory over the broad St. Lawrence, the green Island of Orleans, the white curtain of Montmorency. Off to the north, the rays of morning dance upon the steeple of Charlesbourg and Lorette, pierce the white clouds upon the summits of the Laurentians, and finally disappear in the gloom of the pine forest that marks the limit of cultivation and the beginning of primeval wildness. We glide past the long serpentine form of Beauport, as it lays basking upon shore; the little villages on Orleans, the Isle of Bacchus, as Champlain called it, display their white cottages and tapering spires, they whirl away into distance and give place on the scene to fertile vales and cultivated farms. On our left, the mountains grow larger and bolder, and the huge proportions of Cape Tourmente break the uniformity of blue hills and green roads. The last steeple on the island has just vanished, and the St. Lawrence broadens out before us. From out a wilderness of trees, high over a long stretch of regular fields, behind several mounds, one peak appears to cleave the sky. Above it birds of prey hover in security, at its foot the hamlet of Beaupré reposes—it is the mountain of Ste. Anne. The train suddenly draws up at the little depot on the skirts of the village. We descend, and immediately find ourselves in the midst of another land, in the centre of an age long past. The rude *habitant* carts, the barefooted urchins, and wooden-shod women, the simple primitive Norman costumes, the pleasant manners of the natives, the quaint signboards on the hotels, the hurrying pilgrims and silent devotees, the grotto with its statue and fountain, the convent of the Hospital Nuns on the slope of the hill, the inspiring edifice of the new temple of worship, the long wharf stretching out as it were to catch and hold each passing steamer, the banners,

Interior of the Basilica, Quebec

crosses, processions, and, above all, the religious seriousness of every person, all tell emphatically that we are at last in presence of the world-famed shrine of Ste. Anne-de-Beaupré.

To tell the story of Ste. Anne we must draw upon the Book of Holy Writ, upon history and upon tradition. We will strive to tell briefly who the honored patron of the sacred locality was, and how the spot, so remote from the then known path of civilization, became the focus to which converged so many rays of faith. Two

Montmorency Falls

places, Nazareth and Sephoris—at the foot of Mount Carmel—contend for the honor of being the residence of Ste. Anne. Her husband was Jo-Achim or Eli-Achim. The only offspring of that marriage was Mary, the one destined to become the mother of the Redeemer, and whose name was to be called Blessed by all generations of men. When the mother of the Holy Virgin died, her remains were interred near Jerusalem, in the Valley of Jehoshaphat. From that vale, in the days of the Emperor Trajan, when Christianity was yet but a century old, tradition tells us that a rudderless ship swept over the Mediterranean with the most precious freight ever borne upon that tideless sea. This treasure was the body of Ste. Anne, which was being carried to France and placed in the keeping of St. Auspicius, first bishop of Apt, a town in Provence. It was there that the great Christian monarch, Charlemagne, found it. In after years Ste. Anne became the patroness of Britanny, and at Auray a shrine was built in her honor, and the faith of the simple Breton taught that she there performed miraculous cures for all who trusted in her.

From Niagara to the Sea.

It was in 1608 that Samuel de Champlain founded the city of Quebec. A few years later, a crew of Breton sailors were buffetted most unmercifully by a terrific tempest; all hope seemed to have fled; all earthly succour was despaired of; when, naturally, they turned to the protection of their people, and they vowed to build a shrine in honor of

A Street in the Village of Ste. Anne-de-Beaupré.

Ste. Anne-d'Auray, should she guide them safely through the storm. They landed at last, under her protection, at the spot where now stands the beautiful basilica. They built a little chapel in fulfilment of their promise. In 1660 it became necessary to rebuild the unsubstantial edifice — a primitive one indeed it was—and a Mr. Etienne Lessard gave the land necessary for the purpose. At that time a Sulpician father — de Quen — was parish priest of Quebec, and he deputed Rev. Mr. Vignal to go and bless the corner stone of the new church. The then governor of New France, M. d'Ailleboust, went down to the ceremony, and officially presided at the laying of the foundation of the first shrine to Ste. Anne in Canada. There were then only ten churches in the country. In 1770 the chapter of Carcassonne, in France, sent out a relic of St. Anne, to be kept in the new shrine. Rich presents came from the court of Louis XIV and the queen-mother — Anne of Austria embroidered a chasuble for the service of Ste. Anne's new altar.

These were days of great faith and great glory ; this was the age when the spirit of heroism had been revived by Turenne ; the spark of chivalry had been stirred up by Condé ; exploits of navigators and explorers were repeated from lip to lip ; voyageurs brought back stories of the wonderful shrine upon the banks of the majestic St. Lawrence ; religious fervor and national enthusiasm combined to lavish gifts upon the humble church that stood amidst primeval grandeur upon the confines of a new world. The Marquis de Tracey, vice-roy of New France, had vowed, in the hour of shipwreck, to lay a gift at the feet of Ste. Anne. He fulfilled his compact by presenting a painting by the famed artist Lebrun, representing Ste. Anne and two pilgrims. It hangs over the high altar of the church, and beneath it are the arms of the donor. Bishop Laval de Montmorency gave two pictures from the brush of Luc Lefrançois, a Franciscan friar, and a silver reliquary set in precious stones. In 1706 Lemoine d'Iberville, the heroic pioneer soldier, presented the massive silver crucifix now on the altar. Previous to 1866 the magnificent new church was erected, also an auxiliary chapel built with the materials, and having the decorations, steeple and bell, of the primitive church, was placed at the north side of the large temple. The new church is two hundred feet long, one hundred and five feet broad, fifty-six feet high internally, and has a number of lateral chapels and a large sacristy. It was solemnly blessed and opened for public worship on the 17th of October, 1876.

Island of Orleans, below Quebec

It was consecrated, with imposing ceremonies, upon the 16th of May, 1889, by His Eminence Cardinal Taschereau. Two years after its completion—1878—it was placed under the charge of the Redemptorist Fathers. It is of Corinthian architecture, and its twin towers rise to a height of one hundred and sixty-eight feet. Over

Bay St. Paul, below Quebec

the doorway, between the steeples, is a colossal statue of Ste. Anne, which is fourteen feet high and of exceptional beauty. On entering, the traveler is impressed by the richness and grandeur of the temple, as well as surprised at the novel... all he beholds. At either side of the main entrance are pyramids of crutches and various surgical appliances that have been left by those who found relief from their infirmities and sufferings. One might easily spend a pleasant day examining the beautiful paintings, diving into the lateral chapels, watching the processions of "the lame, the halt and the blind" coming and going, and taking in scenes that cannot be duplicated on the American continent. In 1889 the number of pilgrims ran up to nearly one hundred thousand, and in 1897 there were one hundred and twenty-three thousand four hundred and fifty-five who passed in and out of that temple. It has only been within the last twenty or thirty years that pilgrims have carried away the water from the little fountain, but marvellous efficacy is attached to it. As to the authenticity of the miracles performed at the shrine of St. Anne we are not prepared to speak, nor is it within the scope of our present purpose. But whether the wonderful cures—hundreds of which are as well authenticated as any fact of history—are due to the miraculous intervention of the saint, or to the faith of the devotees, or to natural causes that have never been explained, still the cold, undeniable, glaring facts are there. The lame have thrown away their crutches and have walked, the blind have recovered their power of vision, the paralytic have been relieved of their sufferings, and numberless other infirmities have disappeared at Ste. Anne-de-Beaupré. The writer witnessed one case—of an invalid who had not walked for years and was carried on a chair to the altar-rails—and the result was astounding. The infirm pilgrim arose, at a given moment, from the chair, even as if the Son of God had repeated His words: "Arise, take up thy bed and walk."

It matters not with what preconceived ideas you approach this sacred place, whether you believe or disbelieve in the intercession of the saint and in the miraculous effects of the prayers offered up, you cannot fail to be stirred into emotion by all the surroundings. If the traveller be a Roman Catholic, he finds something sublimely unusual in a pilgrimage to a sacred shrine: he is wafted back to the "Ages of Faith," when the pilgrim, with staff in hand and cross on breast, trod the weary and lengthy paths that led to the centres of devotion: he feels an indescribable inspiration in the presence of so much fervor, so much evidence of sincerity and its reward: he bends

Murray Bay

before the altar, in presence of a pyramid of crutches, canes and other objects that tell of the hundreds of cures operated, and he rises up a better man, a truer Christian, with higher ideals, loftier conceptions. If the tourist be a non-Catholic, he cannot fail to admire

Rivière du Loup.

the simple faith of the numerous pilgrims that he will meet at the shrine, he must see in it all a something so unlike our matter-of-fact electric and steam-working age, that it leads him back irresistibly into past ages. He there beholds what he might never adequately comprehend—the fervor with which millions have been filled by enthusiastic preachers of holy pilgrimages ; he can satiate the most craving appetite for the mystic. Even were the excursionist an unbeliever—an atheist—he must be impressed in some way or other by a visit to Ste. Anne-de-Beaupré. The traveller who goes to Ste. Anne for devout purposes most decidedly has chosen the proper route and the proper terminus ; the one who visits the place through curiosity is certain to have full and entire satisfaction, and may rely that in leaving he will have felt perfectly contented with the trip ; the person who undertakes the journey, no matter with what motive or with what intention, and who has eyes to see and ears to hear, as well as an imagination to be kindled, and a soul to be stirred into life, must return home thankful that, before his voyage of life has drawn to a close, he has enjoyed a real education and excursion combined.

With Ste. Anne's closes the description of the interesting spots in the vicinity of Quebec, and embarking on board the Saguenay River palace steamboat the journey seaward is continued.

From the opening of navigation to June 15th, steamers leave Quebec for the Saguenay and intermediate ports on Tuesdays and Saturdays at 8 a.m.

From June 15th to July 8th the splendid steamers "Carolina" and "Canada" will leave on Tuesdays, Wednesdays, Fridays and Saturdays, and from July 8th until August 20th, inclusive, daily at 8 a.m.

From August 20th to September 16th, steamers leave Tuesdays, Wednesdays, Fridays and Saturdays, and from September 16th to close of navigation, on Tuesdays and Saturdays at 8 a.m.

The steamers leave Chicoutimi the day following their departure from Quebec.

Leaving the Island of Orleans on our left, we glide along past picturesque villages, pointed spires, towering hills, on towards the Cape of Tourmentes and the region so rich in folk-lore. Château Richer and the blue peak of Mount Ste. Anne appear in the distance, and soon Grosse-Isle, the quarantine station of the St. Lawrence,

Thatched Barn, Cape Tourmente.

where, in 1847-48, thousands of emigrants perished during a frightful rage of fever, is passed. From here the river begins to expand, and the broad, open waters seem to have the proportions of a sea. Soon come in view Baie St. Paul and Isle-aux-Coudres. In 1663

Steamer "Canada" arriving at Cap-à-l'Aigle.

Baie St. Paul was the scene of a fierce elemental war. For six months and a half shocks were felt throughout Canada. Along the St. Lawrence meteors filled the air, which was dark with smoke and cinders, the grass withered and crops would not grow. New lakes were formed and the appearance of the shore was altered, and a hill descended into the waters and emerged to form an island. Isle-aux-Coudres has its legend gathering round the memory of Père La Brosse, the faithful priest of the Hudson's Bay post at Tadousac. The legend runs that the priest, one evening, while conversing with his little flock, told them that at midnight he would be a corpse, and at that hour the bell of the chapel would toll for the passing soul. He told them not to touch his body, but to hasten, whatever the weather, on the following day, to Isle-aux-Coudres to fetch Messieur Compain, who would be waiting for them, to wrap his body in its shroud. At the first stroke of midnight the little band was startled by the tolling of the bell, and on rushing to the church they found the priest dead before the altar. With dawn came a violent storm, but, faithful to their promise, they set out for Isle-aux-Coudres, where, as foretold, Father Compain was waiting, breviary in hand, having been warned in a vision and by the tolling of the bell of his own chapel. For years after, the Indians, going up and down the Saguenay, never passed Tadousac without praying in the church where reposed the body of him who had been to them the image of their Heavenly Father. Prostrating themselves on his tomb, and placing their mouths at a little orifice made in the floor of the choir, they talked to him as in life, in perfect confidence. The ingenuousness and simplicity of the faith of these swarthy Montagnais is a touching monument to Père La Brosse. The relics of Père La Brosse, whose memory is revered to this day, were removed many years ago to the church at Chicoutimi.

All along this route a series of wild and rugged grandeur is presented to view, forming a fitting prelude to the wondrous splendor of the Saguenay.

Murray Bay is a favorite watering-place of the lower St. Lawrence. The village is picturesquely situated amid frowning hills and wild scenery; it is an incomparable summer resort for the fashionable world, the comfortable hotels, well-furnished and well-arranged boarding-houses, and the numerous cottages which are rented to visitors, giving a varied choice of accommodation. Here also is a

Tadousac, from Saguenay River

valuable mineral spring, whose waters are highly recommended to invalids; it possesses also good sea-bathing and clear, bracing air. It is renowned as a sporting place, both for anglers and field sports, surrounded by numerous lakes, all well stocked with the reputed trout usually supplied on board the Company's Saguenay steamers. Some miles below Murray Bay the Pilgrims are seen. They consist of a remarkable group of rocks, which, from their height, are visible at a great distance, the "mirage" seeming constantly to dwell about them, due to refraction of the sun's rays, owing to the rocks being sparsely covered with vegetation.

Steaming across the river, it is evening when that beautiful summer resort, Rivière-du-Loup, five miles from the famed watering-place, Cacouna, the Newport of Canada, is reached.

On the Beach, Cacouna.

Cacouna is one of the leading watering-places on the lower St. Lawrence. It is the seat of an old French parish, preserving the ancient customs of old France. It is placed on an elevation above the sea and facing the west; having a beautiful ever-green slope to the salt-water beaches. The St. Lawrence here is twenty miles wide, with the bold Laurentian mountains forming the opposite shore, which, with the remarkably pure air, produces most beautiful sunsets and is surrounded with lovely views as far as the eye can reach. The magnificent shade-trees and groves, lawns, play-grounds and promenades, driving on the fine roads, inland or on shore, boating, sailing and fishing, form some of its many attractions.

Cacouna is a favorite resort for Canadian and American families, who have erected here neat and tasty cottages for their summer homes.

Its salubrity, elevation and average summer temperature, as well as salt sea breezes and balmy air, make it specially attractive.

St. Lawrence Hall, Cacouna.

Many physicians prescribe a summer residence in this part of the country to such of their patients as are subject to general debility and lassitude resulting from life in low latitudes.

Sea-bathing, one of the principal recreations, with a smooth and gentle sloping beach and no undertow with the tide, is made perfectly safe.

The Cacouna Athletic and Gentlemen Riders' Club annual meeting is an attractive feature at this place, for lovers of field sports.

The atmosphere is dry and temperature even.

Cacouna has an elegant and spacious hotel, the St. Lawrence Hall, open for guests from June to September. It has been so extended and improved that it is now one of the most commodious seaside hotels in the Dominion. The bed-rooms are large, comfortable and well ventilated, several being *en suite*, while almost every room in the house commands a magnificent view of the river or surrounding country. It is supplied with billiard-room, bowling-alley, concert-hall, and elegant parlors. Its extensive dining-room is airy and well lighted. The *cuisine* is unsurpassed, being under the supervision of a competent French *chef*.

Across the river, twenty odd miles, is the town of Tadousac, at the mouth of the Saguenay. Tadousac was the first settlement made by the French on the St. Lawrence. It was their principal fur-trading post, and the large revenues from this trade were a prolific source of contention during most of the time in which the kings of France held sway in Canada. As the fur-bearing animals, however, disappeared, so did the commercial and political glory of Tadousac, and now a quiet hamlet, still glorious in its surroundings, is what is left of the former life of this historic spot.

There is a very pleasant and comfortable hotel here, which is

St. Lawrence Hall, from the Sea

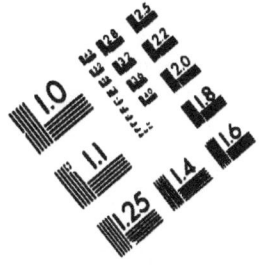 

**IMAGE EVALUATION
TEST TARGET (MT-3)**

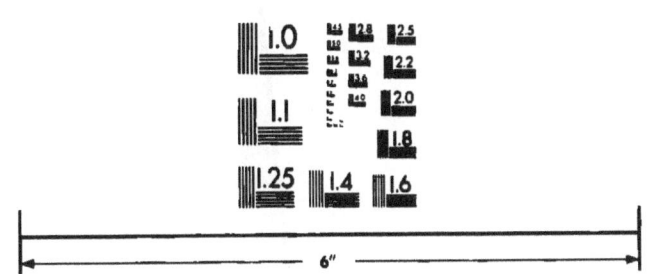

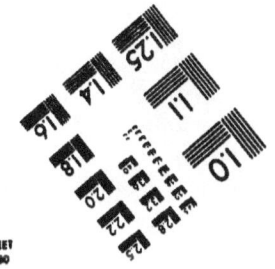

Photographic
Sciences
Corporation

23 WEST MAIN STREET
WEBSTER, N.Y. 14580
(716) 872-4503

well patronized. It is owned and operated by the Richelieu and Ontario Navigation Company, lighted by electricity and with the latest modern improvements. Golf has been added to the outdoor sports for the amusement of guests. The atmosphere at this locality is especially bracing; the salt air from the Gulf of St. Lawrence and the breezes

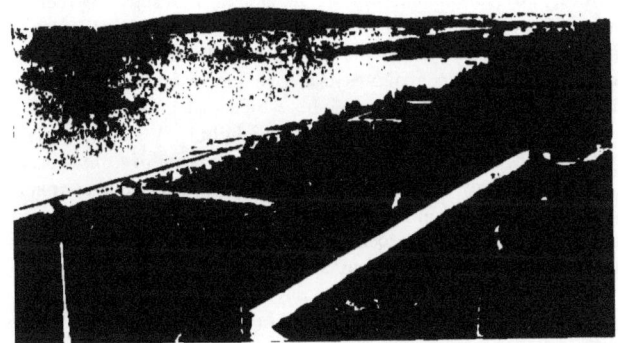

View from St. Lawrence Hall, Cacouna.

from the Saguenay hills meet here, and probably at no place in North America can the denizens from heated localities find greater relief or lay in a larger amount of health than at Tadousac. Time is given to walk over and visit the village, including the little church, the first ever built in Canada, and at half-past eight the steamer prepares to face the mysteries of the world-famed Saguenay, and enter a scene which pen has never yet adequately described. No one can realize this picture all at once; everything is deceptive, and it takes time to grasp the magnitude of the surroundings. But by degrees the immensity and appalling grandeur of the environments assert themselves, and the beholder feels and knows that he is in close communion with the awful majesty of nature. Here, above all other places, the grandest works of man sink into insignificance, and the very silence seems to do homage as to a god. Calm and unbroken is the solitude of nature in this her temple. Mirth and laughter may ripple over the waters, but she heeds them not. Storms and tempests may rage around, and the sun's fierce rays descend upon her brow, seeking to disturb her serenity ; but in vain. Victorious in some elemental conflict, she ceases from her labors. Peace, inviolate, is the guerdon of her warfare, and the loneliness of her grandeur the highest monument of her triumph.

Thus we are made to feel as the seclusion of these waters is penetrated. At every turn some new and unexpected beauty meets the eye, distinct, bearing the stamp of individuality, and yet, in some mysterious manner, inseparable from the whole. There are, however, no rivals among these gorgeous scenes. Projecting rock and sheltered cove, fir-crowned cliff and open bay, each to the other lends a charm, and each reiterates the same grand theme. Even the silent bosom of the waters contributes its meed of praise, for in their unfathomable depths are mirrored the heights which soar into the infinite.

Who can picture this scene by moonlight? Vision is replaced by feeling. Yonder in the distance a silvery beam of light seems to have lost its way among these frowning sentinels, and to tremble in their keeping. On we glide through its fairy-like shadows into darkness again, and the rocks appear to bar our progress. But no ; still we move, and wonder only succeeds wonder.

But let us change the scene to daylight, in the golden glory of a summer's day. As the vessel moves onward, the multiform rocks, the bays and projections, the perpendicular walls, slanting sides and overhanging cliffs, all change with the rapidity of a kaleidoscopic view. But there is no monotony, only increasing loveliness. From the summit of these rocks, crowned with sunshine, to the depths of the transparent waters, all is beauty and deep and lasting peace.

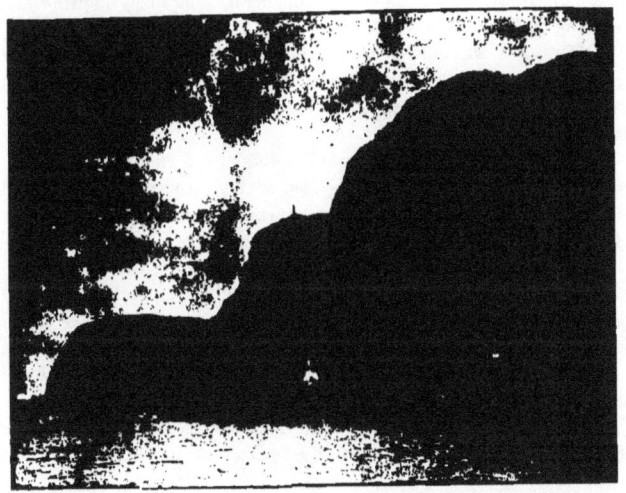

Capes Trinity and Eternity, Saguenay River.

The scene grows upon you hour by hour, until you seem to form a part and share in this wondrous manifestation of nature. The shades contrasted with the sunlight form beautiful combinations, but when the shadow of Cape Eternity falls upon the surrounding slopes, as if the sun had withdrawn its light, while high above is seen its glittering crown, a picture is formed which no words can paint, for no scene will ever replace that formed under the shadows of Cape Eternity.

But our journey is not yet ended. On we pass, surrounded by nature in her wildest moods, until appear once more the scenes of civilization. The sight of the beautiful open water known as Ha! Ha! Bay comes as a relief after the majesty we have left behind us. The bay was named, so the story runs, from the surprised laugh of the earliest French explorers, who, sailing, as they thought, straight up the river, found themselves in this huge cul-de-sac. A scattered, picturesque village decks the shore, and the tourist will meet with an interesting type of Canadian character in the villagers. A short drive through a romantic country, enjoying the breeze of the pine-clad hills, or a sail in the steamer round the bend of the river, will bring us to Chicoutimi.

Beautifully situated on a hill, Chicoutimi seems to form a little world of its own. Its name appears to be singularly appropriate, meaning in Cree "Up to here it is deep."

Chicoutimi was one of the earliest Jesuit missions, and a great fur-trading centre, becoming afterwards one of the principal posts of the Hudson's Bay Company, and it could boast of a church as early as 1670.

Chicoutimi has now a splendid aqueduct system, and is illuminated by electric light. There is also a very large pulp mill, which is supplied with water power by means of a flume having a diameter of $11\frac{1}{2}$ feet.

Its newly enlarged hotel now bears the name of the Château Saguenay. It is lighted by electricity, and is as comfortable and homelike as a traveller would wish.

We are near the famous hunting and fishing grounds of the Saguenay region. Tourists who wish to reach the paradise of wildwood sport, in the vicinity of Lake St. John, may take their passage at Chicoutimi *via* the Quebec and Lake St. John Railway, as the Richelieu steamers connect with the trains on this line.

Chicoutimi, showing Ste. Anne Saguenay River.

The beautiful and fertile region of the lake continues to attract sportsmen to its shores. Here are the homes and haunts of the land-locked salmon, rejoicing in the euphonious Indian of Ouan-anische, and may well be described as a mailed warrior of surpassing courage and determination when he takes the hook. Dear to the true hunter, he is not only a good fighter in the water, but a delicately delicious guest at the table.

Good fishing is to be had anywhere on the rivers and lakes of the gloriously diversified region around Lake St. John. And there large game—deer, bear, moose and the wapiti—are to be found in season, with capable and companionable guides to lead the hunter to their native fastnesses. Nowhere in the world will the sportsman and the lover of the grand and beautiful in nature find better rewards for his toil. Many American, as well as Canadian, fishing clubs, have leases, or own lakes among these hills. But there is room for thousands more; the country is so vast and its lakes and rivers simply inexhaustible. There are good hotels and every accommodation to be had in the villages around Lake St. John. Guides and canoes are available there for sportsmen, and an elegant steel steamer, the "Mistassini," having a capacity for four hundred passengers, runs daily between Roberval and the fishing grounds on the other side of Lake St. John.

It is time, however, to return to our steamer. Leaving Chicoutimi behind, we pass again through magnificent scenery, which is still further impressed on our memory. Rapidly we glide by the long procession of headland, rock and hill, the scattered hamlets, the silver threads of cascades here and there trickling down dark precipices, until, towards evening, we approach the rocky nooks of Tadousac. We can just distinguish in the starlight the massive wooden pier and the lofty pines before us. In a short time we are fairly out of the Saguenay and enter the wide expanse of the St. Lawrence, which we cross to Rivière-du-Loup.

Rivière-du-Loup is the stopping place for passengers for Cacouna. The steamers recross again to Murray Bay, and in the morning we find ourselves again in Quebec, with a whole day before us, which will afford ample time to visit the picturesque suburbs of

Quebec. A point of particular interest within pleasant driving distance is the site of the old hunting lodge of the Intendant Bigot, beyond the village of Charlesbourg. All that now remain of the building known as Château Bigot are the weather-beaten walls, in an open glade beside a stream, with a few bushes which indicate the presence of a garden. Here the wicked intendant was wont to hold his carousals with his boon companions of the hunt, after the fashion pictured in *Le Chien d'Or*. The building has its legend of a buried hoard of silver, and of a beautiful Huron girl, who loved Bigot and died a violent death.

Another very enjoyable trip, through open and fertile country, may be made to the Indian village of Lorette, inhabited by a remnant of the Huron tribe, and where the last traces of this primitive race are to be found.

Hotel Victoria, Quebec.

In the house of one of the chiefs is preserved a portrait bestowed by royal hands on a former chief.

A charming drive, nine miles below Quebec, leads to the Falls of Montmorency.

The old, long, quaint village of Beauport, where may still be seen the remants of Montcalm's forts—and in the centre of which is the famous asylum—stretches nearly the whole distance. Like a large pre-historic monster, it lies along the shore of the river, its head resting upon the bridge over the St. Charles, and its tail lashing into foam the wonderful Falls of Montmorency. It would be impossible to give an accurate description of the beauty, the majesty, the thundering might of those falls, either in winter or in summer. Down a precipice of over two hundred feet, the Montmorency River plunges into the St. Lawrence, and, as if recoiling after its terrible fall, it bends back in spray that, when frozen, leaves a cone fifty feet high, in winter, between the torrent behind and the sheet of ice in front. We must not forget to visit the Island of Orleans, the summer residence of so many Quebeckers. It is a charming sail down stream, during which we get a panoramic view of Quebec, Beauport and the Montmorency Falls on one side and Lévis on the other.

An enjoyable day may be spent visiting either of the places mentioned, while those who prefer to remain in the city will find many new and interesting features.

In the evening the steamer leaves for Montreal, and a pleasant night's sail up the St. Lawrence, with restful sleep, lands the traveller in Montreal in the early morning.

Montreal is happily typical of Canada, for, besides being the commercial metropolis of the Dominion, from its position at the head of ocean navigation, it still retains in its streets and its inhabitants, many traces of French and English occupation. Here the Old World mingles with the New, and the rapid strides of progress seem only to make the contrast more apparent. It is not only to the Canadian tourist that Montreal appeals with special interest; visitors from the sister country will find amid its memorials much which speaks to them of their own country, and many a link that binds them in a friendly bond of union.

Montreal.

The accompanying little sketch and illustrations will serve to assist in a tour of inspection, and be worthy of preservation as a souvenir of a visit to the metropolis of Canada. The first place to visit is the Custom House, a short distance to the west of the Richelieu and Ontario Navigation Company's wharves. Our mission is not to decide any question of tariff, but to view the cradle of Montreal. Affixed to this building are two tablets which read as follows: "This site was selected and named, in 1611, 'La Place Royale,' by Samuel de Champlain, the founder of Canada," and "Near this spot, on the 18th day of May, 1642, landed the founders of Montreal, commanded by Paul de Chomedey, sieur de Maisonneuve; their first proceeding being a religious service."

The city, it is seen, was founded in 1642, by Paul de Chomedey, a knight of the mediæval school, who was accompanied by a Jesuit, Father Vimont. While in the vicinity, it may be interesting to learn something of the ceremony attending the foundation. As eve approached, Maisonneuve and his followers assembled at the place indicated by yonder obelisk, where the first mass was sung. History has preserved part of that early scene in these words: "Tents were

Bonsecours Church, Montreal

pitched, camp fires were lighted, evening fell, and mass was held. Fireflies caught and imprisoned in a phial upon the altar served as lights, and the little band was solemnly addressed by Vimont in words which included these: 'You are a grain of mustard-seed that shall rise and grow till its branches overshadow the earth. You are few, but your work is the work of God. His smile is upon you, and your children shall fill the land.'" Such, then, were the beginnings of the city, and the foundation of the educational and commercial system which, in the space of two hundred and fifty years, has changed the aspect of this vast country.

There is, however, an earlier period, which takes us back into the ages of discovery, gathering around the name of Jacques Cartier, without which no description of Montreal would be complete. In 1535 Jacques Cartier, shortly after his discovery of Quebec, sailed up the St. Lawrence in search of the kingdom of Hochelaga, of which he had received glowing accounts from the Indians of Stadacona. On the 2nd of October the exploring party, consisting of about fifty sailors and their officers, in a small galleon and two longboats, approached the shores of the mysterious kingdom. An Indian path led through the forest to the fortified town or kingdom of Hochelaga, situated at the base of the mountain. All trace of this village, however, had disappeared at the time of Champlain's visit, and its inhabitants had either been massacred or carried away into captivity during the war after Jacques Cartier's visit.

The history of the war between the Iroquois and Hurons has been preserved by a descendant of the latter tribe, from whom it is learned that the Hurons and Senecas lived in peace and friendship for many a generation at the town of Hochelaga. They intermarried and had no cause for quarrel, till, for some reason, a Seneca chief refused his son permission to wed a maiden of the other tribe. Enraged at the action of the stern parent, the lady refused all offers of marriage, declaring that she would only wed the warrior who should slay the chief who had interfered with her happiness. A young Wyandotte, smitten by her charms, attacked and slew the old chief, and received the coveted reward. The Senecas, however, adopted the cause of their chief, and a terrible fratricidal war spread desolation throughout the Huron country, nor did it cease until the Iroquois had completely broken and exterminated the Hurons. The story of the heroine has been compared to that of Helen, and the fate of Hochelaga to the siege of Troy.

While in this vicinity, Bonsecours Church and Bonsecours Market claim attention. The church of Notre-Dame-de-Bonsecours, from which the adjoining market derives its name, is, to the antiquarian, of the deepest interest. Its foundation dates from 1657, only fifteen years after the foundation of the city, when de Maisonneuve donated a piece of land on which to build a chapel. The first building measured thirty by forty feet, but it was soon found to be too small, and in 1675 a larger church was commenced, which stood until its destruction by fire in 1754. The present church was commenced soon after, but not completed until 1771. There are many old paintings in the church, to which great value is attached, but the principal object is the time-honored statue of the Blessed Virgin. This was acquired by Sister Mary Bourgeois from a noble of Britany,

Montreal Harbor.

where it was reputed for miracles. She, in consequence, brought it over, built the chapel for it, and set it up where it now stands, and where it has remained the patron of the French sailors for nearly two centuries and a half. Bonsecours Market is specially worthy of a visit on one of its market days. Here an illustration of the

Custom House, Montreal.

provincial life of the *habitant* may be obtained. To the observer of human nature, the *habitant* and his methods of doing business will furnish an interesting study.

In the midst of the St. Lawrence, nearly opposite the market, is a favorite resort in summer, known as St. Helen's Island, named by Champlain after his wife. The island is laid out as a park, and, being thickly wooded, has many shaded walks. Within an enclosure contain' a fort is a space reserved for military purposes. The island is reached by the boats of the Richelieu and Ontario Navigation Company.

To enable the tourist to take in at a glance the magnificence of the city's situation, it is necessary to visit the Mountain Park. Ascending the mountain by the inclined railway or by a series of winding roads, a glimpse is obtained here and there through the foliage of the panorama spread out below ; but it is not till the summit is reached that an idea of the vastness of the scene is realized. It was from this point that Jacques Cartier viewed the fertile country he had come to claim for France, when, uplifting the cross, he gave to it the name of Mount Royal.

"Therefrom one sees very far," he wrote, and his words are re-echoed to-day. On one side stretches out the city, with its spires and domes glittering in the sun, the palatial homes of the wealthy, the meaner dwellings of the poor ; broad avenues and parks and tokens of industry, and beyond, Nature's watery highway lined with docks and shipping, the prosperous towns and villages which rise from its southern shore. And turning, through the shadow of the trees, may be seen the beautiful and silent city of the dead.

It may be observed that with the rise of commerce the city has crept nearer and nearer to the foot of the mountain. For fifty years after its foundation the limits of the town were strictly confined within fortified walls, on account of the frequent attacks of the Indians, but as they were subdued or civilized, suburbs sprang up outside of these boundaries.

We may trace the recognition of Montreal as a commercial centre as being largely

City Hall, Montreal.

due to the operations of the North-West Company. This association of wealthy French Canadian and Scottish merchants made their headquarters in the town, while developing the fur trade in the Far West, and their activity and enterprise did much to build up the commercial fabric of Canada.

The advantageous position thus obtained has become permanent, for, backed by the great lake and canal systems which connect it with Chicago, Duluth and other cities, its influence pierces far into the interior, and the Canadian Pacific Railroad, with headquarters in Montreal, brings the commerce of India and China and the Canadian West across the continent. In the year 1672 the population of Montreal was one thousand five hundred and twenty, and an idea of the progress made in fifty years may be gleaned from the fact that about this time the village of

Post Office, Montreal.

Laprairie, on the southern shore, was founded by a band of Christian Iroquois. A hundred years later, in 1770, is found the following description: "Montreal is situated on an island of that name, the second place in Canada for extent, buildings and strength. The streets are regular, forming an oblong square, and the houses are well built. The city has six or seven gates, large and small, but its fortifications are mean and inconsiderable. The inhabitants, about five thousand, are gay and lively, and more attached to dress and finery than those of Quebec, and, from the number of silk sacks, laced coats and powdered heads that are constantly seen in the streets, a stranger would imagine that Montreal was wholly inhabited by people of independent fortunes." As the present population is about three hundred thousand, considerable progress is manifest since 1770. For a long time Commissioners street, on the water front, was the great business thoroughfare; then St. Paul street doffed its private character and assumed a commercial aspect. Later on, business found its way into Notre-Dame street, and thence into St. James street, but here its limitations were marked for many years. At this time Craig street was an open ditch, that surrounded the old fortifications of the city. This, in time, was filled up and transformed into a broad avenue, and then trade crept still further north. Within the past few years St. Catherine street, so long devoted to private residences, has become the centre of great activity, and dwellings are constantly being converted into stores. Important improvements have been completed by the municipal authorities within the past ten years that contribute to the beauty and facilities of the city. Nearly all the streets have been paved, and several of the leading thoroughfares have been widened. There has also been a notable increase of buildings erected by corporations and business firms. Among these may be mentioned the stations of the Grand Trunk and Canadian Pacific railways, both of which were comparatively insignificant buildings until within this period. On St. James street, in particular, several handsome structures have been completed, including the lofty building of the New York Life Insurance Company, at the corner of Place d'Armes; the Temple Building, on the site of the pioneer St. James Methodist church; the Canada Life Insurance Company's building, at the corner of St. Peter street, and the Bank of Toronto, at the

The Bank of Montreal.

corner of McGill street, wherein the consul for the United States has his offices; while the Imperial building, the Mechanics' Institute, and the City and District Savings Bank buildings have undergone extensive alterations. On Notre-Dame street the Sun Life Insurance Company's offices and the Balmoral Hotel have been added to the list of large buildings, and on St. Catherine street the most important structures erected within this period are St. James Methodist Church, Morgan's dry goods store, Henry Birks & Sons' building, and Murphy's and Ogilvy's buildings. The Montreal Street Railway, on the corner of Craig street and Place d'Armes hill, have also a fine office building. A corresponding activity has been noticeable in the erection of private dwellings, and many stately homes, which have been completed within the past few years, are proof of the prosperity of the city.

Old Seminary Gate and Clock, Montreal.

Descending the mountain road, we pass under the elevator on the eastern slope, and, gaining the main road, leave the Exhibition Grounds on the left, and cross what is known as Fletcher's field. The large stone building facing us, with its prominent dome, is the Hôtel-Dieu, Saint-Joseph-de-Ville-Marie. It was first founded over two hundred and fifty years ago, by the Duchess de Bullion, and much of the early history of Montreal is bound up with it. Turning into Pine avenue, there is a good view of the buildings of the Royal Victoria Hospital, the joint gift of Lord Strathcona and Mount Royal and Lord Mount Stephen. It is constructed on the most approved plans, equipped with all modern appliances, and recognized as one of the leading hospitals on the continent.

Driving down McTavish street, a good view of the Reservoir is obtained, and soon the interesting buildings of McGill are seen.

The de Maisonneuve Monument, Place d'Armes, Montreal.

From Niagara to the Sea.

McGill University. The grounds and buildings of McGill College occupy a part of the ancient town of Hochelaga. A tablet on Metcalfe street, in front of the western portion, reads thus: "Site of large Indian village, claimed to be the town of Hochelaga, visited by Jacques Cartier, 1535." The university owes its origin to Hon. James McGill, who, by his will, dated 8th January, 1811, devised the estate of Burnside, consisting of forty-seven acres

Victoria Square, Montreal.

of land, with the manor-house, and buildings thereon erected, and also bequeathed the sum of ten thousand pounds sterling to the Royal Institution of Learning to establish a university to be distinguished by the appellation of McGill. With the proceeds of this estate the present institution was commenced, and a royal charter obtained in 1821, and reorganized by an amended charter in 1852. The William Molson Hall, being the west wing of the college building, was erected in 1861, by the donation of Mr. William Molson. The Peter Redpath Museum was donated to the university, in 1880, by Mr. Redpath. In 1890 Mr. W. C. McDonald gave the McDonald Physics building and its equipment to the university, which is one of the most valuable additions to McGill, and in the same year the Redpath Library was added as a gift of Mr. Peter Redpath. The Donalda building is the gift of Lord Strathcona, as a college for the higher education of women.

There are also a large number of endowed chairs, and endowment for pension fund, and a number of exhibitions and scholarships There are fifty professorships and thirty lecturership on the staff of the university in the faculties of Arts, Applied Science, Medicine, Law, Comparative Medicine, and Veterinary Science. The Peter Redpath Museum contains large and valuable collections in botany, zoology, mineralogy and geology, arranged in such a manner as to facilitate work in these departments.

Within a few minutes' drive from McGill, on Sherbrooke street, are the substantial buildings and ample grounds of Montreal College, under the direction of the Sulpicians. This is one of the best classical colleges in America. In connection with it is the Grand Seminary, and recently a new school of philosophy has been erected on the hill, near the botanical gardens, to accommodate the increasing number of students. From this college priests have gone forth into almost every diocese of the United States. Close to the entrance of the new building may be seen the ruins of Capitulation House, which is asserted by tradition to have been the headquarters of General Amherst when he occupied the heights on approaching to the siege of Montreal, then a small town miles away. A tablet also marks it thus: "Tradition

McGill University and Grounds, Sherbrooke Street, Montreal.

asserts that the capitulation of Montreal and Canada was signed here, 1760."

From the mountain, and during the drive, we have been able to form an idea of the extent as well as the aspect of the city. It now

Montreal College.

remains for us to direct attention to the numerous buildings and institutions that are calculated to prove of interest.

The Laval University. The Laval University is to the French what McGill is to the English—their principal seat of learning. The chief seat of Laval, however, is at Quebec. It rose out of the Seminary of Quebec, founded by Mgr. Laval, a princely prelate, who endowed the institution with his vast wealth. The university charter is dated 1852, and therein it is given the name of its founder. The lectures of the faculties in Montreal have hitherto been delivered in various buildings scattered over the city, but recently a new and handsome building has been erected on St. Denis street.

Montreal's Public Buildings. Amongst Montreal's most interesting buildings is the Château de Ramezay—one of the oldest historical landmarks—associated with events of the greatest importance in Canadian history. It was built in 1705 by Claude de Ramezay, governor of Montreal. Within its venerable walls, after the fall of Quebec, in 1760, arrangements were completed for the withdrawal of the last French garrison from Montreal, by which act the finest colony of France, and for which the French had done so much, became the possession of Britain.

In 1775 the château was again made memorable as the headquarters of the American Brigadier-General Wooster, and in the following year, under General Benedict Arnold, the Commissioners of Congress, Benjamin Franklin, Samuel Chase, and Charles Carroll of Carrolton, here held council. To Benjamin Franklin Montreal was indebted for its first printer--Fleury Mesplet, who established *The Gazette*, which is still in existence as one of the leading papers of the city.

For years after the British conquest, the château was recognized as the official residence of English governors while here. For a time a portion of the building was used as the Circuit Court, but is now converted into a museum, in which repose many interesting souvenirs associated with the history of Canada. A visit to the spacious vaults will give an idea of the stability of the structure, which could not be obtained from exterior view.

Eastwards is the old Quebec Gate Barracks, now utilized as a railway station, and on Craig street are the famed Viger Gardens, opposite which the new hotel and station has been erected by the Canadian Pacific Railway Company.

To the west of the City Hall is situated the Court House, recently enlarged to meet the legal requirements of Montreal and the district. Affixed to this building is a tablet bearing this inscription: "Here stood the church, chapel and residence of the Jesuit Fathers. Built 1692; occupied as military headquarters 1800; burnt 1803. Charlevoix and Lafitau, amongst others, sojourned here. On the square, in front, four Iroquois suffered death by fire, in reprisal, by order of Frontenac, 1696."

This square was also, during the present century, the site of the town pillory, so that the administration

Laval University, Montreal.

of justice, in various forms, seems to have been meted out on this spot from the earliest to the present time. The north side of the Court House overlooks a large open space, known as the Champ de Mars, still used as a military parade-ground. The soldiers of France and British troops have both trod this historic ground. East of the Court House is the City Hall, a handsome structure of grey cut stone. From the tower a fine view is to be obtained.

Art Association Building, Montreal.

The Board of Trade, on St. Sacrament street, is probably the largest public building in the city. It is a fine solid structure of red stone, six storeys in height and well laid out. Many of the large manufacturers and corporations have offices in the building. The Board's exchange hall occupies an area of over four thousand square feet, while the safety vaults beneath cover an area of three thousand square feet.

The Post Office, on St. James street, is built in French Renaissance style, and has recently been altered to meet the requirements of the city, but it is still considered too small for the vast amount of business transacted.

Place d'Armes. In this square, past and present interests are united. On the north side is the Bank of Montreal, one of the wealthiest institutions on the continent, having a capital of twelve million and a reserve fund of six million dollars. The style of its architecture, of the Corinthian order, forms a pleasing contrast to the buildings which surround it. The sculpture of the pediment, representing Canadian scenes, is the work of Mr. Steel, R.S.A. Some of the frescoes of the interior are considered very fine, and should be seen. The northern boundary of the city, in 1721, extended as far as this building, the stone fortifications running through its side.

Facing the bank, on the south side, is the parish church of Notre-Dame, with its two impressive towers, which rise to a height of two hundred and twenty-seven feet. The length of the church is two hundred and fifty-five feet, with a breadth of one hundred and thirty-five feet, and a seating capacity of fourteen thousand. To see this vast edifice crowded, as it is on important festivals of the Church, such as midnight mass at Christmas and similar occasions, is a most imposing spectacle.

A chapel at the south-east of the church has been recently constructed, and is a beautiful specimen of ecclesiastical architecture. The view obtained from the west tower is a remarkable one; on a clear day, in the far distance, may be seen the hills of Vermont. The great bell, named *Gros Bourdon*, weighing 24,780 lbs., one of the five largest bells in the world, is also located in this tower. Many fine specimens of art are to be found in the church, which is open at all times. Adjoining the church is the Seminary of St. Sulpice, which is interesting as preserving the ancient style of architecture of the building of the city. Many curious volumes are to be found in the library of the seminary, one of special interest being the first parish register of the church, in which the signature of de Maisonneuve, the founder of Montreal, frequently occurs.

On the eastern corner of the square is a tablet reading thus: "In 1675 here lived Daniel de Grésolon, Sieur Duluth, one of the explorers of the Upper Mississippi, after whom the city of Duluth was named."

A little further east is the site of the house of the founder of another American city, distinguished by a tablet reading: "In 1694 here stood the house of La Mothe Cadillac, the founder of Detroit."

The whole of the ground in this vicinity possesses a charm for the antiquarian and historian. The centre of the square, now adorned

Château de Ramezay, Montreal.

by a monument to the founder, was once the scene of a battle.
The event is recalled by an inscription on a building to the east of
the Bank of Montreal: "Near this square, afterwards named
La Place d'Armes, the founders of Ville-Marie first encountered
the Iroquois, whom they defeated; Chomedy de Maisonneuve
killing the chief with his own hands, 30th March, 1644." The

Mount Royal Park Drive, Montreal.

monument, unveiled recently, illustrates some of the principal events
in the founder's career, and also perpetuates the memory of several
of his contemporaries.

Dominion Square. On this square, picturesquely situated, are many of
the important buildings of Montreal. The Windsor,
one of the best hotels in Canada, occupies a commanding site at the
corner of Dorchester street. The hotel is thoroughly equipped, and
provides accommodation for seven hundred guests. A large hall
adjoining, with a seating capacity of sixteen hundred, is utilized as
a ball-room and as a hall for private or public receptions. Both in
winter and summer, a large amount of business is done, and in past
years, when the winter carnival was on the square, a splendid view
of the ice palace and other buildings could be obtained from the

windows of the hotel. Facing the southeast corner of the hotel is the Macdonald memorial, erected to the memory of the late Honorable Sir John A. Macdonald, prime minister of Canada, and one of the "fathers of Confederation." The monument was unveiled on the 6th of June, 1895, by Lord Aberdeen, then governor-general. The bronze figure under the canopy represents the Premier in the robes of a Grand Commander of the Bath, of which order he was a member. The canopy is crowned with the figure of Canada, encircled by the nine provinces of the Dominion. The bas-relief panels are illustrative of Canadian history. The figures were designed and modelled by Mr. Wade, an English sculptor.

At the south-east of the square, facing Dorchester street, is St. James Cathedral, claimed to be the largest church on the continent. The foundations were commenced in 1870, and much of the work is still incomplete. The ground plan of the cathedral is designed in the form of a cross, three hundred and thirty feet long and two hundred and twenty-two feet wide, after the model of St. Peter's at Rome.

The dome, which always attracts visitors, is seventy feet in diameter and rises to a height of two hundred and ten feet inside, while the extreme height to the top of the cross is two hundred and fifty feet. Adjoining the cathedral on the south is the palace of the Roman Catholic Archbishop of Montreal.

Windsor Hotel, Montreal.

Facing the west end of the cathedral, on Dorchester street, is the new stone and brick structure of the Young Men's Christian Association. The appointments of this building are very complete, and it has a large membership.

Located at the south-west of the square is the massive grey stone building of the Canadian Pacific Railway. The exterior appearance would scarcely indicate that it was the terminus of a modern railroad : its substantial tower and turrets, with their ancient loopholes, suggesting rather the days of feudal might. However, any such illusion is immediately dispelled on going into the interior, where the luxurious waiting-rooms and admirably arranged offices point to the highest civilization of the nineteenth century. At the foot of the hill is the handsome red brick building, the principal station of the Grand Trunk Railway. The spacious offices of this company are, however, located at Point St. Charles.

Balmoral Hotel, Montreal.

Within a few minutes' drive of the square, on Dorchester street, is a building always attractive to visitors—the Grey Nuns' Hospital. It was founded in 1747, by Madame de Youville, the widow of an officer. Many objects of interest are to be seen here, such as the personal belongings of the foundress. There is also a legendary interest attached to portions of the grounds. The story of the red cross, which is to be seen at the corner of Dorchester street, takes us back to the days of the rack, for it is said to mark the grave of one who, after conviction of murder and robbery, was condemned to be broken alive.

In "Montreal after Two Hundred and Fifty Years," by Mr. Lighthall, we find that the punishment inflicted on this unfortunate individual was as follows: "He was condemned to torture, ordinary and extraordinary, and then to have his arms, legs, thighs and reins broken, alive, on a scaffold to be erected in the market-place of the city, then put on a rack, his face towards the sky, to be left to die."

The daughter of the founder of the State of Vermont, Ethan Allen, was a member of the order of the Grey Nuns, and there is a pretty legend connected with her and a picture of St. Joseph which led her to finally adopt the vows of the sisterhood.

The Natural History Society Museum, situated on University street, off St. Catherine, is a small, unpretentious building, but it will undoubtedly prove interesting to many of our visitors. The library is rich in scientific lore, while many priceless collections are to be found in the museum. The Ferrier collection of Egyptian antiquities is probably the most perfect in America. The Natural History Society, which publishes the *Canadian Record of Science*, has its headquarters in this building.

The Art Gallery, located on Phillips Square, contains a fine collection, in which Canadian art is well represented, but frequently loan exhibitions are held here, when works are on view from the private galleries of wealthy citizens. Some of the most valuable pictures in the world are the property of Montrealers.

The only public library in Montreal is the Fraser Institute, on Dorchester street. The number of volumes is somewhat small, though the selection is good. In the French section there are many exceedingly valuable works.

Montreal is known far and wide as the city of churches, and there are many others besides those we have already mentioned that are worthy of inspection.

Christ Church Cathedral, on St. Catherine street, is a fine specimen of Gothic architecture, and its proportions are very beautiful.

On Bleury street is the Church of the Gesu, built after the plan of the Gesu at Rome, from a design by Mr. Keely, of Brooklyn, N. Y. It was consecra-

St. James Cathedral, Montreal.

ted on December 3rd, 1865. The edifice is one hundred and ninety-two feet in length, and one hundred and forty-four feet wide at the transept; the height in the centre is seventy-five feet. The towers, which will be the principal external attraction, have not yet been built. There is a profusion of altars on both sides of the church and in the niches and corners. The paintings of the Gesu are, however, the great attraction for all visitors.

Royal Victoria Hospital, Montreal

St. Patrick's Church is one of the finest structures in the city. It is *par excellence* the shrine where the Irish Catholics worship. It is surrounded by extensive grounds. The church is under the direction of the members of St. Sulpice, and its aisles have witnessed some of the most imposing ceremonies ever beheld in Montreal.

On St. Catherine street, immediately east of St. Denis, is the gem-like church of Notre-Dame-de-Lourdes. This was built in 1874. It was erected in honor of the Immaculate Conception and of the apparition of the Blessed Virgin to Bernadetta Soubirous, in the Grotto of Lourdes, in the Upper Pyrénées.

To the Numismatic and Antiquarian Society of Montreal we are indebted for the numerous tablets which, with their inscriptions, indicate places of historic interest that would otherwise be lost sight of.

At the corner of St. Peter and St. Paul streets a tablet is affixed to a building, the inscription of which reads as follows: "Here lived Robert Cavalier, Sieur de La Salle, 1668."

Ancient Buildings, etc. The name of La Salle stands out boldly in history, and reference has been made to him previously in connection with the village of Lachine. To Americans and Canadians his deeds appeal with equal force. Of him the late Francis Parkman, of Boston, wrote: "Beset by a throng of enemies, he stands, like the King of Israel, head and shoulders over all. He was a tower of adamant, against whose impregnable front hardship and danger, the rage of man and the elements, the southern sun, the northern blast, fatigue, famine and disease, delays, disappointments and deferred hopes, emptied their quivers in vain. The very pride which, Coriolanus-like, declared itself most sternly in the thickest press of foes, has in it something to challenge admiration. Never, under the impenetrable mail of paladin or crusader, beat a heart of more intrepid metal than within the stoic panoply that armed the breast of La Salle. America owes him an enduring memory, for in his masculine figure she sees the pioneer who guided her to her richest heritage." La Salle met with a tragic fate, being assassinated by two of his followers, in Louisiana, in 1687.

Another house that will interest visitors from the sister country is situated on the south-east corner of St. Peter and Notre-Dame streets. It is an old-fashioned building, but it was once the most magnificent dwelling in the city, with grounds extending across Notre-Dame and St. James streets and terminating at Craig street. It was here that the gallant American, General Montgomery, took up his headquarters in 1755, and it was afterwards occupied by Generals Wooster and Arnold, of the United States army. The interior decoration appears to have been very elaborate, for we find this description: "The principal rooms were wainscotted up to a certain height, and above that, tapestried richly with scenes from the life of Louis XIV. A tablet fixed to the building reads: "Forrester

House. Here General Montgomery resided during the winter of 1775-76."

Another site that appeals to tourists is located on St. Paul street, between Place Royale and St. Sulpice street, as being the birthplace of Pierre LeMoine, in 1661. It was he who conquered the Hudson's Bay for France, in 1697, and who discovered the mouth of the Mississippi, 1699. In 1700 he was elected first governor of Louisiana. His brother, who founded New Orleans, in 1717, and was afterwards governor of Louisiana for forty years, was born in this house.

De Catalogne House, on St. Vincent street, is memorable as the home of one of the earliest engineers of Montreal. An inscription on the building reads: "1693. House of Gédéon de Catalogne, engineer, officer and chronicler. Projector of the earliest Lachine Canal."

Christ Church Cathedral, Montreal.

"Beside the dark Uttawa's stream,
two hundred years ago,
A wondrous feat of arms was wrought which all the world should know."

In an old French street, off St. James street, between St. Peter and McGill streets, known as Dollard lane, is a tablet reading: "To Adam Dollard des Ormeaux, who, with sixteen colonists, four Algonquins and one Huron, sacrificed their lives at the Long Sault of the Ottawa, 21st May, 1660, and saved the colony."

Adam Dollard.

The story of the heroism of Dollard has been told over and over again in prose and verse, and is familiar to a large number of Americans thereby.

Montreal is famous for its athletic clubs. The largest body of athletes is the Montreal Amateur Athletic Association, whose magnificent grounds are situated on St. Catherine street west, on the direct line of the street cars. The national game is lacrosse, which

View on Sherbrooke Street, Montreal, looking West.

is carried to greater perfection here than elsewhere. The Shamrock Amateur Athletic Association have recently opened up their beautiful grounds in the north of the city. The Montreal Hunt Club have a fine pack of hounds, which may be seen at the kennels. As

the winter is the season for sports, when the skating rinks and curling clubs are in full swing, very little idea can be obtained at the present time of the extent or of the enthusiasm with which the various sports are indulged in.

We wish to mention, before closing, the Jacques Cartier Hotel, situated on the square of that name. It is in the very heart of the city, and commends itself to the travelling public as a resort where comfort may be had at reasonable rates. The hotel is conducted both on the American and European plan.

From Montreal the tourist can make many charming excursions.

To any one desirous of spending a pleasant week on the water, and at the same time visit a few of the largest cities and towns in Canada, the trip from Montreal to Hamilton, and return, has no equal. The splendid steel steamer "Hamilton" leaves her wharf, in the Canal basin, foot of McGill street, every Thursday afternoon, at four o'clock, returning to Montreal the following Wednesday. Sunday is spent in the "ambitious city" of Hamilton, which is situated at the extreme western end of Lake Ontario. A very pleasant day can be spent here; the hotel accommodation is first-class. The New Royal Hotel is, without doubt, the handsomest and best built hotel in the city. It has been renovated and newly decorated and fitted up this year, and is now one of the finest hotels in Canada. Messrs. Patterson & Paisley are the proprietors, which in itself is a recommendation for good service and all that may be desired in a modern hotel.

One of the finest trips which the Province of Ontario affords is one through the grand scenery and magnificent vistas of that great eastern arm of Lake Huron, the Georgian Bay. It is estimated that there are more than thirty thousand islands of every description lying in this great water expanse. It is not only the scenery, fishing and other sporting attractions that entice tourists to these parts, but good hotel accommodation, where travellers and summer resorters may find all that is desired in a first-class and up-to-date hotel. Among the best hotel properties in the Georgian Bay district are Canada's great summer hotel, the Penetanguishene, which is beautifully situated on the Georgian Bay, at Penetang; the Sans Souci, at the mouth of the Moon River, and the Belvidere, at Parry Sound. The Penetanguishene accommodates about three hundred guests, is electric lighted, steam heated, and has all the modern improvements. Good boating, bathing and fishing is enjoyed here. The Sans Souci is on the steamer route, the mail boat calling here twice daily. It is in the centre of the greatest fishing and hunting grounds in the Georgian Bay district, with black bass and maskinongé in abundance. The Belvidere, at Parry Sound, is situated on a high eminence overlooking the waters of the sound, and is an ideal spot for the tourist. The hotel is newly fitted up, and everything has been done to make it first-class in every respect.

To those who have leisure at their disposal, we would suggest a visit to the capital of the Dominion, the city of Ottawa. The capital is beautifully situated on the banks of the Ottawa River, and may

Ottawa. be reached from Montreal by the Canada Atlantic and Canadian Pacific railways, both modern and well-equipped lines, or, if preferable, by the boats of the Ottawa River Navigation Company. By rail or water, the scenery obtainable during the journey is pleasing. Ottawa is the centre of the great lumbering interests of the Dominion, where one may watch the huge logs as they are deftly drawn out

The New Royal Hotel, Hamilton.

of the water and converted in a few minutes into saleable lumber, ready for the markets of America and Europe.

Visitors may also experience the novelty of descending the slides, whereby the hardships of the lumberman's life, for a few exciting moments, becomes the attractive sport of venturesome seekers of strange thrills.

The Russell, Ottawa

The descent of the slides is a feature so peculiar to the city, that all her illustrious visitors have been introduced to its charms, as a matter of course, and have thereby been initiated into the craft of the raftsman. Apart from the various scenes connected with the lumbering industry, the principal feature of the city is the Parliament and Departmental buildings. The first stone of these handsome buildings, which cover an area of over four acres, was laid by the Prince of Wales, in 1860.

The buildings form three sides of a huge square, which is laid down in grass, beautifully kept, whose fresh green surface, crossed by broad paths, stands above the level of Wellington street, from which it is separated by a handsome railing.

Rising above this square, on a stone terrace, the central block, with a massive tower two hundred and twenty feet high in the centre, faces the square. This building contains the two Chambers; one for the Senate and the other for the Commons. Behind the Chambers is situated the Parliamentary Library, a building of exceptional architectural grace. It is fitted with every convenience, and is admirably arranged for reading purposes. The collection of the library is exceedingly valuable. Running entirely around the

The Gilmour, Ottawa.

three block of the Parliament buildings is a broad drive, and at the sides and in the rear of the Library the grounds are laid out in well-planted beds, with great stretches of green lawn overlooking the cliffs. From here a commanding view is obtained of the Ottawa River. The drives in the vicinity of Ottawa are charming. About two miles from the city is Rideau Hall, the residence of the Governor-General. The city is up-to-date in every way, it has an excellent electric railway system and several first-class hotels.

The Russell Hotel is one that has become known throughout the world. It is the leading hotel in the city of Ottawa, and statesmen and prominent men from all parts make it their home while in the city. The appointments and internal arrangements are modern and up-to-date, and comfort, with unsurpassed service, is assured to all its patrons.

The Gilmour, a comparatively new hotel, has been well furnished, and is under able management. The *cuisine* is all that can be desired, and nothing is left undone for the comfort of the guests.

The Grand Union is another hotel that is recommended. Large airy rooms, with good attendance and all modern conveniences. Rates moderate.

The Windsor, situated in a central part of the city, is patronized by members of Parliament and prominent men of Canada. It is attractively decorated and furnished, and is run, under experienced hotel managers, in a manner that pleases all who stop at this hostelry.

Another enjoyable trip can be made from Montreal, *via* the Delaware & Hudson Railway, to Saratoga and Albany. This trip brings the tourist along the beautiful shores of Lake Champlain, past the palatial Hotel Champlain, at Bluff Point, where a very delightful stop can be made, and on to Saratoga, which, with its immense hotels and handsome private residences, its beautiful shaded promenades and boulevards, its magnificent parks and phenomenal mineral springs, its brilliant social and literary entertainments,

Drinking the Waters at Congress Spring, Saratoga, N.Y.

enjoys a greater distinction than any other watering place on the American continent, and annually attracts a host of visitors from every country of the civilized world to contribute to its gayety. Representatives of the most diverse nationalities may be seen sipping the crystal medicinal waters, side by side, while on the broad piazzas all languages are spoken. Its various mineral waters are known all over the world. Prominent among these may be mentioned the Congress Spring Water. This famous water being now (by a most elaborate retubing) restored to all its former strength and excellence, the great mineral-water-drinking public might have been seen, the past season at Saratoga, hurrying to slake their thirst at this healthful fountain. While the water is now as strongly cathartic as at any period since its discovery—over one hundred years ago—it still retains the delicious flavor and smooth cathartic action that has always been its characteristic.

The golf links in connection with the hotel are the finest in the country. The season commences about June 15th, and closes the early part of October.

As to hotel accommodation, Saratoga is unsurpassed on the continent. Pre-eminent stands the United States, one of the finest and best known summer hotels in the world, with accommodation for fifteen hundred guests.

Saratoga possesses charms peculiarly its own, and those who have been there can readily understand the expression, "There is but one Saratoga."

From Saratoga to Albany is a short run of thirty-nine miles, and from there a network of railways and steamboat lines give the tourist a choice of routes. The Hotel Kenmore, in Albany, is a really fine house, conveniently situated and with all modern improvements.

Among the most needed additions to the city of Albany, N.Y., which 1899 has brought forth is the new Hotel Ten Eyck. The structure is the highest building in the city, and is a monument to the enterprising citizens who have secured for Albany a modern first-class hotel. The hotel is under the management of Messrs. H. J. Rockwell & Son, and is conducted on both the American and European plan.

The Hotel Empire, corner of Boulevard and Sixty-third street, New York city, is a modern first-class, fire-proof hotel, conducted under practical management, for the accommodation of those who want the best at a reasonable cost. The *élite* of travellers and tourists from all parts of the world make this hotel their headquarters while in New York. It is also famous for the perfection of its *cuisine* and service, its artistic and home-like appointments, and the

The United States Hotel, Saratoga, N.Y.

splendid location of its site. It is also within a few minutes of the leading theatres and close to the retail business portion of the city. Street cars running to all parts of the city pass the door.

The Fuller Company of Detroit, Mich., is one of the leading electrical supply concerns in America, and its business extends to all parts of the country. The finest and best passenger steamers

The Kenmore, Albany, N.Y.

plying the Great Lakes and the River St. Lawrence are equipped with the Fuller dynamos, and the ship signal apparatus furnished by this concern is the one most approved of by the steamboat companies, and one which is most extensively used. Steel plate blowers for forced draft motors, fans, etc., are specialties manufactured by the Fuller Company, and recognized as second to none in the market.

The Dominion Atlantic Railway's service during the coming summer between Boston, Halifax and St. John, N.B., by means of its unrivalled fleet of steamships, and its Pullman palace car "Flying Bluenose" express, will supply the only route worthy of patronage. It will give the maximum of pleasure at a minimum cost, and will give hundreds of thousands a readily available opportunity of spending glorious summer days in the unequalled vacation lands of Nova Scotia and New Brunswick. Two additional magnificent nineteen-knot twin-screw ocean liners have been added to the service, and are known as the "Prince George" and "Prince Arthur." The Dominion Atlantic Railway management have decided to better their own record. They have already revolutionized the methods of passenger travel between Boston and the Maritime Provinces of Canada; and what more delightful trip can be imagined than by this excellent service? Effective care has been taken for the safety of these ships, and the latest and most approved devices have been placed on these boats, including search-lights and Hatfield's steering-gear, which is only found on battleships and cruisers. Each vessel is able to sleep three hundred and eighty-two passengers.

A direct fortnightly steamship service between Halifax, N.S., and London, Eng., and between Halifax and Liverpool, *via* St. John's, Nfld., will be operated this summer by the well-known and popular Furness lines. Fast, full-powered, high-class, Clyde-built steamships have been placed on these routes, and a quick service, with every comfort, is assured passengers by this line. Steamers will sail from Halifax to London every alternate Thursday, and from Halifax to Liverpool every alternate Wednesday, the steamships on the latter route calling at St. John's, Nfld. The rates of passage between Halifax and London range from $45.00 to $60.00, and from Halifax to Liverpool from $45.00 to $50.00, according to location.

Parliament Buildings, Ottawa.

Superior accommodation for first class passengers is assured, and all the steamers carry a stewardess. The London steamers carry a doctor. The saloon and sleeping apartments are placed amidships, are well ventilated, and secure to passengers the greatest luxury and comfort at sea, including fresh air, with the minimum of motion. The steamships are electric lighted throughout. All information as to sailing dates, rates and other particulars may be had from the agents, Messrs. Furness, Withy & Co., Ltd., People's Bank Buildings, Halifax, N.S.

The Northern Michigan Transportation Company's new steel steamship "Illinois," running between Chicago and Mackinac Island, will make two trips a week each, leaving Chicago on Wednesdays at 1.00 p.m. and Saturdays at 4.00 p.m., arriving at Mackinac Island on Thursdays at 8.30 p.m. and Mondays at 6.00 a.m.; returning leave Mackinac Island on Thursdays at 10.00 p.m. and Mondays at 8.00 p.m., arriving at Chicago on Saturdays at 6.30 a.m. and Wednesdays at 6.30 a.m.

Before saying *au revoir* to the tourist, we wish to draw his attention to the hotels, railways and supply houses who are advertisers in this book. None but first-class houses have been accepted for these pages, and travellers can depend on the reliability of the firms whom we recommend.

This Guide is printed upon "PHOTO BOOK" paper, specially made by the Canada Paper Company, Montreal and Toronto.

FRY'S CHOCOLATES

ARE SOLD ON BOARD OF ALL TRAINS AND ON ALL RICHELIEU & ONTARIO NAVIGATION COMPANY'S STEAMERS.

—— ASK FOR THEM.

Wholesale Agents:

D. MASSON & CO.
MONTREAL.

Save the Duty by buying DIAMONDS

IN CANADA.

Unset Diamonds enter Canada free of duty, and are therefore much cheaper than in the United States.

You buy here almost as closely as traders buy to sell again — more closely than some traders buy.

Fine grades exclusively.

Mounted on the premises.

HENRY BIRKS & SONS,

BY SPECIAL APPOINTMENT
JEWELLERS TO THEIR EXCELLENCIES
THE GOVERNOR-GENERAL AND
THE COUNTESS OF MINTO.

PHILLIPS SQUARE,

MONTREAL.

ESTABLISHED 1831.

John Henderson & Co.

···FURRIERS···

No. 229 St. James Street,

MONTREAL.

We carry the largest and richest **FUR STOCK** in the Dominion. Visitors to Montreal are invited to call and inspect our **Fur Display**.

Show Rooms open at all seasons.

Correspondence solicited from Fur Buyers at a distance.

JOHN HENDERSON & CO.

The Splendid Record of the I.O.F.

THE BENEFITS PAID.

Benefits paid last Year (1898) $1,176,125 14
Benefits paid last Five Years 4,185,455 15
Benefits paid last Ten Years 5,482,460 72
Benefits paid from 17th June, 1874, to 31st Dec., 1898 . . 6,279,992 84

THE GROWTH OF THE MEMBERSHIP.

Membership 1st July, 1881 369   Date of Reorganisation.
Membership 31st December 1881 . . 1,019   Increase in Six Months . . . 650
Membership 31st December, 1886 . . 5,804 Increase in First Five Years . . 4,785
Membership 31st December, 1891 . . 32,303 Increase in Second Five Years . 26,499
Membership 31st December, 1896 . . 112,838 Increase in Third Five Years . . 80,535
Membership 31st December, 1898 . . 137,128 Increase during Year 1898 . . . 21,290

THE INCREASES DURING 1898.

Increase of Benefits Paid . . . . . . $ 183,890 54
Increase of Premium Income 192,660 48
Increase of Total Income 262,660 12
Increase of Net Assets 100,000 00
Increase of Surplus Funds 627,537 58
Increase of Assurance in Force 20,113,500 00

THE EXPANSION OF THE SURPLUS.

Surplus 1st July, 1881 . . . . . . $ Date of Reorganisation.
Surplus 31st December, 1881 . . . 4,865 55 Increase in Six Months . . . . $ 4,865 55
Surplus 31st December, 1886 . . . 53,581 28 Increase in First Five Years . . 48,412 73
Surplus 31st December, 1891 . . . 408,708 28 Increase in Second Five Years . 355,110 00
Surplus 31st December, 1896 . . . 1,559,454 18 Increase in Third Five Years . 1,560,956 18
Surplus 31st December, 1898 . . . 2,189,576 96 Increase during Year 1898 . . . 627,537 58

For further information respecting the I.O.F. apply to any Officer or Member.

EXECUTIVE COUNCIL:

ORONHYATEKHA, M.D., S.C.R., Toronto, Canada.
HON. JUDGE WEDDERBURN, P.S.C.R., Hampton, N.B., Canada.
VICTOR MORIN, S.V.C.R., Montreal, Can.
JOHN A. McGILLIVRAY, Q.C., S.S., Toronto, Canada
H. A. COLLINS, S.T., Toronto, Canada
T. MILLMAN, M.D., M.R.C.S., Eng., S. Phy., Toronto, Canada.
E. G. STEVENSON, S.C., Detroit, Mich

HEAD OFFICE:
The Temple Building, corner Richmond and Bay Sts., Toronto, Can.

OFFICE FOR EUROPE 24 Charing Cross, LONDON, ENGLAND.
OFFICE FOR UNITED STATES 6436 Kimbark Ave., CHICAGO, ILL.
OFFICE FOR THE PACIFIC COAST Phelan Bldg., 806 Market St., SAN FRANCISCO, CAL.

TOURIST RATES.

FROM NIAGARA FALLS TO	SINGLE	RETURN
Toronto	$1.50	$2.25
Kingston	6.35	10.50
Clayton	6.35	10.50
Alexandria Bay	6.85	11.25
Montreal	11.25	19.00
Quebec	14.25	24.00
Murray Bay	16.65	28.00
Rivière-du-Loup	16.65	28.00
Tadousac	17.25	29.00
Chicoutimi, Ha ! Ha ! Bay, Saguenay River	18.25	31.00
Roberval (boat to Chicoutimi, thence rail)		34.00
Roberval (up rail, down boat)		34.00

FROM TORONTO TO		
Charlotte	2.50	4.00
Kingston	5.00	8.50
Clayton, Alexandria Bay and Thousand Island Park	5.00	9.00
Stanley Island	8.00	13.50
Montreal	10.00	†16.70
Abenakis Springs		*17.00
Quebec	13.00	*20.00
Murray Bay, Rivière-du-Loup	15.40	*24.00
Tadousac	16.00	*25.00
Chicoutimi, Ha ! Ha ! Bay, Saguenay River	17.00	*27.00
Roberval (boat to Chicoutimi, thence rail)		*30.00
Roberval (up rail, down boat)		*30.00
Gaspé, Que , R. & O. to Quebec, thence Quebec SS. Co.	23.00	*37.00
Percé, Que., do do	24.00	*38.70
Summerside, P. E. I., do do	28.00	*45.50
Charlottetown, P. E. I., do do	29.50	*48.05
Pictou, N. S., do do	30.00	*48.90
Boston, R. & O. to Montreal, thence rail	19.00	
R. & O. to Quebec and return to Montreal, thence rail	24.00	
R. & O. to Quebec, thence rail	24.00	
New York, R. & O. to Montreal, thence rail	20.65	
R. & O. to Clayton, thence rail	13.80	
R. & O. to Montreal, thence via Lakes Champlain and George, and rail	22.15	
R. & O. to Montreal thence via Newport and Springfield	20.00	
R. & O. to Quebec and return to Montreal, thence rail	25.00	
R. & O. to Quebec, thence rail	25.00	

EAST.

FROM MONTREAL TO		
Abenakis Springs		2.00
Quebec	3.00	5.00
" (going Saturday, returning Sunday)		3.00
Murray Bay, Rivière-du-Loup	5.40	9.00
Tadousac	6.00	10.00

* An additional charge of $5.00 will be made for passengers returning by rail from Montreal, Kingston or intermediate points.
† An additional charge of $1.30 will be made for passengers returning by rail from Montreal, Kingston or intermediate points.

TOURIST RATES—Continued.

EAST.

FROM MONTREAL TO			SINGLE	RETURN
Saguenay			$7.00	$12.00
Roberval (boat to Chicoutimi, thence rail)				15.00
Roberval (up rail, down boat)				15.00
Cacouna (boat to Lévis, and Intercolonial Railway			5.60	9.30
Little Metis	do	do	7.40	11.60
Metapedia	do	do	9.25	14.40
Dalhousie	do	do	9.75	15.10
Moncton	do	do	13.00	21.00
Pointe-du-Chêne	do	do	13.00	21.50
St. John	do	do	13.00	21.00
Halifax	do	do	15.00	25.00
Pictou	do	do	15.00	25.00
Sydney	do	do	18.00	27.50
Boston (boat to Quebec, thence rail)			14.00	
New York	do		15.00	

WEST.

	SINGLE	RETURN
Alexandria Bay and Thousand Island points	4.50	
Kingston	4.50	8.50
Charlotte, N. Y.	8.50	15.50
Toronto	8.50	‡16.70
New York, N. Y., R. & O. to Clayton, thence rail	12.30	
Niagara Falls, N. Y.:		
Steamer to Toronto, Niagara Nav. Co. to Lewiston, thence N. Y. C. & H. R. R.	10.00	19.00
or steamer to Toronto, Niagara Nav. Co. to Queenston, thence Niagara Falls Park & River Ry.	9.95	19.00
or steamer to Toronto, thence rail	11.25	19.00
Buffalo, steamer to Toronto, thence all routes via Lewiston, or Queenston	10.50	19.00
or steamer to Toronto, thence rail	11.25	19.00
Alpena, Mich., via Toronto, Buffalo, C. & B. T. Co., and Det. & C. Nav. Co.	17.85	30.70
Detroit, Mich., via Toronto, Buffalo, C. & B. T. Co , and Det. & C. Nav. Co.	14.85	26.70
Detroit, Mich., via Toronto, Buffalo, Erie & West. Trans. Co.	17.35	31.70
Cleveland, Ohio, via Toronto, Buffalo, C. & B. T. Co.	13.35	23.70
Cleveland, Ohio, via Toronto, Buffalo, Erie & West. T. Co.	14.85	26.70
Mackinac Island, Mich., via Toronto, Buffalo, Erie & West. Trans. Co.	23.35	44.70
Mackinac Island, Mich., via Toronto, Buffalo, C. & B. T. Co. and Det. & C. Nav. Co.	18.35	31.70
Sault Ste. Marie, Mich., via Toronto, Buffalo, Erie & West. Trans. Co.	23.85	49.70
St. Ignace, Mich., via Toronto, Buffalo, C. & B. T. Co ,and Det. & C. Nav. Co.	18.35	31.70
Duluth, Minn., via Toronto, Buffalo, Erie & West. T. Co.	35.85	69.70
Chicago, Ill., via Toronto, Buffalo, Northern SS. Co. to Mackinac Island, L. M. & L. S. T. Co. SS. " Manitou ".	22.35	39.70
Milwaukee, Wis., via Toronto, Buffalo, Northern SS. Co. to Mackinac Island, L. M. & L. S. T. Co. SS. "Manitou"	22.35	39.70
Milwaukee, Wis., via Toronto, Buffalo, C. & B. T. Co. to Cleveland, Det. & C. Nav. Co. to Mackinac Island, L. M. & L. S. T. Co. SS. " Manitou "	22.35	39.70
Milwaukee, Wis., via Toronto, Buffalo, Erie & West. Trans. Co. to Mackinac Island, L. M. & L. S. T. Co. SS. "Manitou"	27.85	50.70

The Richelieu & Ontario Navigation Co.   135

TOURIST RATES – Continued.

EAST.

RETURN	FROM QUEBEC TO	SINGLE.	RETURN.
$12.00	Murray Bay, Rivière-du-Loup	$2.10	$4.00
15.00	Tadousac	3.00	5.00
15.00	Chicoutimi	4.00	8.00
9.30	Roberval (boat to Chicoutimi, thence rail)		10.00
11.60	Roberval (up rail, down boat)		10.00
14.40			
15.10	**WEST.**		
21.00	Abenakis Springs		4.50
21.50	Montreal	3.00	5.00
21.00	Alexandria Bay and Thousand Island points	7.50	
25.00	Kingston	7.50	13.50
25.00	Charlotte, N.Y.	11.50	20.50
27.50	Toronto	11.50	†20.00
	Niagara Falls, N. Y. :		
	Steamer to Toronto, Niagara Nav. Co. to Lewiston, thence N. Y. C. & H. R. R.	13.00	24.00
	or steamer to Toronto, Niagara Nav. Co. to Queenston, thence Niagara Falls Park & River Ry.	12.95	23.00
8.50	or steamer to Toronto, thence rail	14.25	24.00
15.50	Buffalo : Steamer to Toronto, thence all routes *via* Lewiston, or Queenston	13.50	24.00
‡16.70	Cleveland : Steamer to Toronto, thence all routes *via* Lewiston, Queenston, or to Buffalo, and Cleveland & Buffalo Trans. Co.	16.35	28.70
19.00	Boston : R. & O. to Montreal, thence rail	11.00	18.90
19.00	New York : R. & O. to Montreal, thence rail	12.00	23.00
19.00	R. & O. to Montreal, thence *via* Lakes Champlain and George and rail	13.50	
19.00	R. & O. to Montreal, thence *via* Fabyan's, Boston and rail	16.50	29.00
19.00			
30.70	* An additional charge of $3.00 will be made for passengers using rail train between Montreal, Kingston and intermediate points.		
26.70			
31.70	## ABOUT TICKETS, etc.		
23.70	**Time-Table subject to change with or without notice.**		
26.70	**Passengers are required to exchange their tickets at the Purser's Office before obtaining keys to stateroom.**		
44.70	Half fares charged for children five years of age and under twelve years. Children under five will be carried free.		
31.70	Stop-overs, where allowed, will be granted upon application to Purser.		
49.70	## MEALS AND STATEROOMS.		
31.70	Cleveland & Buffalo Transportation Co.—Extra.		
69.70	Detroit & Cleveland Navigation Co. – Extra.		
	Erie & Western Transportation Co.—Included.		
39.70	Northern Steamship Co.—Extra.		
	Lake Michigan & Lake Superior Transportation Co.—Extra.		
39.70	Quebec Steamship Co. Meals included, berths extra. Berths can be secured by applying to J. G. BROCK, Agent Quebec SS. Co., Montreal.		
39.70	**Richelieu & Ontario Navigation Co.**—Extra. *Exception*—On west-bound tickets reading Montreal to Toronto and intermediate points, when R. & O. N. Co.'s proportion exceeds $3.00, *meals and berths are included*.		
50.70			

STATEROOMS CAN BE SECURED

on application by letter or telegraph to the undersigned Agents, stating clearly number of berths required, from and to what port, and date of starting.

COMPANY'S OFFICES:

J. F. DOLAN, Agent,
   2 King St., East, Toronto, Ont.
L. H. MYRAND, Agent,
   Dalhousie St., Quebec, P.Q.

J. P. HANLEY, Agent,
   Kingston, Ont.
H. FOSTER CHAFFEE, Agent,
   128 St. James St., Montreal.

CONNECTIONS.

HAMILTON.—With Grand Trunk, and Toronto, Hamilton and Buffalo railways.
TORONTO.—With Niagara Navigation Co., Hamilton steamers, and Grand Trunk and Canadian Pacific railways.
CHARLOTTE, N. Y. (PORT OF ROCHESTER)—With N. Y. C. & H. R. R., Lehigh Valley, Erie. Buffalo, Rochester & Pittsburg, Western, N. Y., & Penn., and R. & L. O. Railways.
KINGSTON.—With Grand Trunk and Canadian Pacific through sleepers from the West (trains run to steamboat dock).
GANANOQUE.—With Grand Trunk Railway trains from the West.
CLAYTON.—With New York Central & Hudson River Railway (R. W. & O. Division) through sleepers, and with all steamers for the Thousand Island hotels.
MONTREAL.—With Canadian Pacific, Grand Trunk, Canada Atlantic, Central Vermont, Delaware & Hudson and New York Central railways, for New York, Boston, White Mountain and Adirondack summer resorts.
QUEBEC.—With Intercolonial Railway, and Quebec & Lake St. John Railway, and Quebec Steamship Co.

QUEBEC STEAMSHIP Co.—Steamer "Campana." leaves Quebec fortnightly, commencing Tuesday, May 9th.

HAMILTON, BAY OF QUINTE AND MONTREAL LINE
THROUGH THE BEAUTIFUL SCENERY OF THE
THOUSAND ISLANDS AND BAY OF QUINTE BY DAYLIGHT.
Increased accommodation (Bi-weekly service from June 14).

MONDAYS AND THURSDAYS.		MONDAYS AND THURSDAYS.	
Lve. Hamilton	12.00 noon	Lve. Montreal	1.00 p.m.
Toronto	6.00 p.m.	Valleyfield	1.05 a.m.
Darlington	9.30 "	Cornwall	4.00 "
Port Hope	11.10 "	Morrisburg	9.00 "
Cobourg	12.00 mid.	Iroquois	11.05 "
Brighton	3.00 a.m.	Prescott	1.00 p.m.
Trenton	5.30 "	Brockville	2.15 "
Belleville	7.15 "	Gananoque	5.15 "
Northport	8.30 "	Kingston	10.00 "
Deseronto	9.30 "	Glenora	3.00 a.m.
Picton	11.15 "	Picton	5.30 "
Glenora	12.00 noon	Deseronto	7.30 "
Bath	2.00 p.m.	Northport	8.00 "
Kingston	5.00 "	Belleville	9.00 "
Gananoque	7.45 "	Trenton	10.05 "
Brockville	9.45 "	Brighton	12.00 noon
Prescott	11.00 "	Cobourg	3.00 p.m.
Iroquois	12.15 a.m.	Port Hope	4.00 "
Morrisburg	4.00 "	Darlington	6.00 "
Cornwall	7.00 "	Toronto	9.30 "
Coteau	7.30 "	Arr. Hamilton	2.00 a.m.
Arr. Montreal	12.00 noon		

These steamers also run the Rapids.
Return tickets are good for passage on Daily Mail Line going West on payment of one dollar extra.

Rates of fare are :   Montreal to Hamilton $8.50
                      Montreal to Hamilton and return   16.00

The Richelieu & Ontario Navigation Co.

TORONTO-MONTREAL TOURIST LINE TIME-TABLE.

East-Bound.		West-Bound.	
Lve. Toronto	2.30 p.m.	Lve. Chicoutimi	(According
* Charlotte	18.30 "	Ha! Ha! Bay	(to tide.
† Port Hope	6.00 "	Tadousac	2.30 p.m.
‡ Cobourg	7.00 "	†† Rivière-du-Loup	5.00 "
‡ Kingston	1.15 a.m.	‡‡ Cap à l'Aigle	7.00 "
‡ Gananoque	4.00 "	Murray Bay	10.00 "
‡ Clayton	5.15 "	Arr. Quebec	6.30 a.m.
‡ Round Island	5.45 "	Lve. Quebec	8.30 p.m.
‡ Thousand Island Park	6.35 "	Batiscan	9.30 "
‡ Alexandria Bay	7.05 "	Three Rivers	11.30 "
‡ Brockville	8.35 "	Sorel	2.00 a.m.
‡ Prescott	9.50 "	Arr. Montreal	6.00 "
‡ Cornwall	12.35 p.m.	Lve. Montreal	10.00 "
‡ Stanley Island	2.00 "	Lachine	12.30 p.m.
Arr. Montreal	6.30 "	Valleyfield	6.30 "
Lve. Montreal	7.00 "	Stanley Island	8.30 "
Sorel	11.00 "	Cornwall	9.15 "
Three Rivers	1.30 a.m.	Prescott	8.30 a.m.
Batiscan	2.30 "	Brockville	9.30 "
Arr. Quebec	6.30 "	Alexandria Bay	11.30 a.m.
Lve. Quebec	8.00 "	Thousand Island Park	11.40 "
Murray Bay	2.00 p.m.	Round Island	12.00 noon
Cap-à-l'Aigle	3.00 "	Clayton	12.30 p.m.
Rivière-du-Loup	5.15 "	Kingston	3.00 "
Tadousac	7.45 "	Arr. * Charlotte	9.00 "
Ha! Ha! Bay	(Next morning	Lve. * Charlotte	11.30 "
Arr Chicoutimi	{ according	** Deseronto	6.30 "
	(to tide.	** Belleville	8.30 "
		‡ Cobourg	1.30 a.m.
		‡ Port Hope	2.10 "
		Arr. Toronto	6.00 "

From June 1st to 13th and from September 16th to 30th steamers leave Toronto and Montreal Tuesdays, Thursdays and Saturdays.
‡ From June 14th to July 6th, and from September 3rd to September 15th, daily except Monday.
§ Daily from July 10th to September 3rd.
* Calls Tuesday, Thursday and Saturday.
† Calls Monday, Wednesday and Friday.

†† On Sunday steamer leaves Rivière-du-Loup at 6.00 p.m.
‡‡ Calls during daylight only (weather permitting).
** Calls on Tuesday, Thursday and Saturday.
‡ Calls on Sunday, Wednesday and Friday.
Leaves Brockville at 12 noon on Sunday, Wednesday and Friday.

SUNDAY SERVICE.

Commencing about May 14th, steamers leave Montreal and Quebec at 3 p.m. every Sunday until about October 22nd. Passengers can make convenient connections with steamer going in opposite direction at Three Rivers, both steamers leaving this port at 10 p.m.

SAGUENAY LINE.

From opening of navigation to June 13th, Tuesday and Saturday only; from June 13th to July 8th, Tuesday, Wednesday, Friday and Saturday; from July 8th to August 30th, daily, including Sunday; August 30th to September 16th, Tuesday, Wednesday, Friday and Saturday; from September 16th to close of navigation, Tuesday and Saturday only.
The steamers leave Chicoutimi the day following their departure from Quebec.

RATES FOR MEALS AND BERTHS.
TORONTO TO MONTREAL (going East).

Breakfast or Supper	$0.50	Dinner	$0.75

Staterooms, according to location.
Between Toronto and Montreal, on steamers "Toronto" and "Bohemian," meals are served à la carte, going east.

MONTREAL AND QUEBEC.

Supper or Breakfast		$0.50

Staterooms, according to location.

QUEBEC AND THE SAGUENAY.

Supper or Breakfast	$0.50	Dinner	$0.75

Staterooms according to location.

SIDE LINES.

Montreal to Laprairie, Longueuil, Boucherville, Contrecœur, Chambly and Three Rivers, and up L'Assomption and Yamaska and St. Francis Rivers.

Visitors to Quebec

should not fail
to visit the celebrated

Montmorency Falls

and take a pilgrimage to

Ste. Anne de Beaupré;

to do so take the
...ectric Cars to the

Quebec, Montmorency and Charlevoix Railway Station,

from whence
there are 5 trains daily.

LEADING HOTELS AND BOARDING HOUSES

ALONG THE ROUTE OF

RICHELIEU & ONTARIO NAVIGATION COMPANY,

"NIAGARA TO THE SEA."

HAMILTON.

NEW ROYAL—*Patterson & Paisley,* 79-81 James St. N., 100 rooms, $2.50 to $4 per day.
St. Nicholas—Neil A. McLean 55-8, James St. N , 100 rooms, $1.50 to $2 per day.
Waldorf Hotel—R. M. Gilkison, King St. E., $2 to $3 per day.
    These hotels are all within 3 minutes' walk of the business centre of the city (corner King and James streets). One mile electric cars from port of Hamilton.

TORONTO.

Queens—McGaw & Winnett, 78-92 Front St , 400 rooms, $3 to $4 per day, $17.50 up per week.
Arlington—C. J. Beacham, King and John Sts., 150 rooms, $2 to $4 per day, $12 up per week.
Rossin House—A. & A. Nelson, King and York Sts., 300 rooms, $2.50 to $5 p. day, $17.50 up p. wk.
Walker House—D Walker, Front and York Sts , 400 rooms, $2 to $3.50 p. day, $12 up p. week.
Palmer House—J. C Palmer. King and York Sts , 300 rooms, $2 to $2.50 per day. $10 up per wk.
Iroquois—E. Horseman & Co., King and York Sts., 160 rooms, $1.50 to $2 p. day, spec'l w'k rates
Grand Union—C. A. Campbell, 180 Front St. W , 300 rooms, $1.5 per day, special week rates.
Albion—J. Holderness, 31 Jarvis St., 80 rooms, $1 to $1.50 per day, special rates per week.
Elliot House—J. W. Hirst, Church and Shuter Sts , 100 rooms, $2 per day, $8 to $10 per week.
Somerset House—W. Hopkins, 434 Church St., 80 rooms, $2 per day, special week rates.
Gladstone House—Turnbull Smith, 1202 Queen St. W., 100 rooms, $1 to $1.50 p. day, sp. w'k rates.
Y. W. C. A. (ladies only)—34 Elm St., special week rates
McCarron House—M. McCarron, 23 Queen St. E., 28 rooms, $1 to $1.50 p day, special week rates.
Boarding House—Mrs. J. R. Mason, 16 Spadina Rd , 18 r., $1.25 to $2 p. day, $8 to $18 p. week.
Boarding House—Mrs. Lawlor, 7 Queen's Park St., 22 r., $1.25 to $1.50 p. day, $7 to $12 p. week.
    Accommodation for over 20,000 visitors can be found in the number of good boarding houses all over the city, at $1 per day, or $3 and $5 per week. Cottages in the vicinity of Lorne Park, Hanlan's Point, Balmy Beach, Oakville, Grimsby Park, may be had from $75 to $300 for the season ; apply to Canadian Summer Resort Association, Yonge street, Toronto. Electric cars from Toronto.

BOWMANVILLE.

Bennett House—Bennett & Sons, King St., 30 rooms, $1.50 per day, $3 to $6 per week.
Balmoral—30 rooms, $1.50 per day, $4 to $6 per week
    2 miles' drive (cabs, bus, etc.) from Port Bowmanville to these hotels. Summer cottages to rent on reasonable terms; apply to A. Gulley, J Jeffery or Alan Williams.

PORT HOPE.

St Lawrence—T. E. Branhan, 150 rooms, $2 to $3 per day, $5 to $10 per week.
Queen's—A. A. Adams, 56 rooms, $1.50 to $2 day, $5 to $7 per week
    These hotels are centrally situated at 1/2 mile (cabs) from Port Hope Landing.

COBOURG.

Arlington—Mrs Alexander, 150 rooms, $2 to $2.50 per day, $10 to $12 per week.
Columbian—D. Smith, 38 rooms, $2 per day, $10 to $15 per week.
Dunham—M B Williams, 10 rooms, $1.50 per day, $7 to $10 per week.
    1/4 mile cab drive or walk from port of Cobourg. Cottages may be rented at from $5 to $10 a month.

BRIGHTON.

Central—J. D. Prents, 28 rooms, $1 to $1.50 per day, $5 to $7.50 per week
Proctor—M. J. Alguire, 30 rooms, $1 to $1.50 per day, $5.50 to $7 per week.
    1 1/2 miles' bus drive from port of Brighton to the above hotels. There are several cottages at Presqu Isle Point which may be rented at from $3 to $8 per month each ; reached by boats or busses from port of Brighton.

Leading Hotels and Boarding Houses.

TRENTON.

Gilbert—T. H. Hocker, 40 rooms, $1.50 per day, $5 per week 4 miles' bus drive from port of Canal Bridge.
Summer Resort at Twelve-o'clock Point, along bank of canal H. H. Hunter, prop., Smithfield, Ont.

BELLEVILLE.

Quinte—J. F. Baird, 150 rooms, $2 to $3 per day. Situated on Bridge St., at ¼ mile drive (hack or electric cars) from port of Belleville.
Anglo-American—D. Coyle, 15 rooms, $1 to $1.50 per day, $7 per week, ¼ mile drive.
Kyle House—C. Kyle, 25 rooms, $1 to $1.50 per day, $5 to $6 per week, ¼ mile drive.

There are also numerous boarding houses distributed over the city, ranging from $2.75 to $4 per week.

DESERONTO.

Deseronto House—Wm Hatch 100 rooms, $1.50 to $2 per day, $5 to $10 per week.

PICTON.

Lake-shore House—H. McDonald, Sand Banks, Prince Edward Co., 150 rooms, $1 per day, $5 per week, 10 miles' stage drive from port of Picton.
13 cottages, 4 rooms each, $2.50 per month.
Glen Island—Dingman Bros., Bay of Quinte, 155 rooms, $1 to $1.50 per day, $7 per week, 5 miles from port of Picton (Reindeer stage), ½ mile by small boats from Glenora.
20 cottages, 4 to 7 rooms each, $15 to $25 per month, furnished.
Tecumseh—A. McDonnell, 75 rooms, $1 to $1.50 per day, $5 per week.
Globe—W. H. Vanalstone, 100 rooms, $1 to $1.50 per day, $5 per week, ¼ mile drive.
Royal—Hepburn & Thorn, 100 rooms, $1 to $1.50 per day, $5 per week, ¼ mile drive.

The three above hotels are reached by hacks or bus from port of Picton.

GLENORA.

Glen House—C. A. Cornell 14 rooms, $1 to $1.25 per day, $5 to $7 per week, 100 yards' walk from port of Glenora. Cottages at $5 to $10 per month.

BATH.

Bay Villa—T. Edwards, on the beach, 20 rooms, $1 per day, $7 per week.
This hotel is situated within 150 yards of port of Bath. Boarding houses from $3 to $4 per week.

KINGSTON.

British American Thos. Crate, 125 rooms, $2 to $3 per day, $10 to $15 per week.
Frontenac—Thos. Crate, 125 rooms, $2.50 to $4 per day, $15 to $25 per week.
Anglo-American—A. Stevens, 50 rooms, $1 to $1.50 per day, $5 to $7 per week
City—John Randolph, 75 rooms, $1.50 to $2 per day, $8 to $10 per week.

These hotels are centrally located, within a few blocks from landing, and may be reached by walk or electric cars.

ST. VINCENT.

Union Hotel—20 rooms, $2 per day.
Arlington—10 rooms, $2 per day.
The Anderson—10 rooms, $7 to $10 per week.
Mrs. McConell's 10 rooms, $7 to $10 per week.
Mrs. Frashen—10 rooms, $7 to $10 per week
The Dunning—12 rooms, $7 to $10 week.
McKinley's Riverside—10 rooms, $7 to $10 per week

CLAYTON

Walton House—Thos. Esselstyn, 100 rooms, $2 to $2.5 per day, $14 to $17.50 per week
Hubbard House—Mrs. Hubbard, 150 rooms, $1 to $2, per day, $14 to $17.50 per week.
New Windsor—Mrs. Haas, 75 rooms, $2 to $2.50 per d., $14 to $17.50 per week.

THOUSAND ISLANDS.

Frontenac Hotel—Round Island, 100 rooms, $4 per day.
Pullman House—Sayles, Pullman Island, 100 rooms, $2 to $2.50 per day.
Grand View Park—W. R. Rodgers, Fine View Park, 100 rooms, $2 to $2.50 per day, $12 to $17.50 per week.

Leading Hotels and Boarding Houses.

Columbian Hotel—H. P. Inglehart & Co., Thousand Island Park, 50 rooms, $3 to $4 per day.
New York Cottage—D. L. Bronk, Thousand Island Park, 15 rooms, $7 to $10 per week.
Witherstone Cottage—Mrs. Witherstone, Thousand Island Park, $1.25 per day.
Pine View Hotel—C. C. Pierce, Pine View, 100 rooms, $2 per day, $10 to $14 per week.
Central Park Hotel—Central Park Association, Central Park, 100 rooms, $2 to $3 per day, $12 to $17.50 per week.
Edgewood Park Hotel—J. P. Lawson, Alexandria Bay, 100 rooms, $4 per day.
Thousand Island House—O. G. Staples, Alexandria Bay, 700 rooms, $3 to $5 per day.
Crossman House—C. W. Crossman, Alexandria Bay, 400 rooms, $3 to $5 per day.
Marsden House—P. K. Hayes, Alexandria Bay, 80 rooms, $2 to $3.50 per day.
Jefferson House—Z. Bigness, Alexandria Bay, 100 rooms, $2 per day.
Westminster Hotel—H. P. Inglehart, Westminster Park, 250 rooms, $2.50 to $3 per day.
Grenadier Island Hotel—Jos. Senécal, Rockport, Ont., 50 rooms, $1.50 per day.
Cedar Island—W. K. Wylie, Chippewa Bay, 60 rooms, $1.50 per day.

GANANOQUE.

Gananoque Inn—St. Lawrence River, 100 rooms, $3 to $5 per day, $12 to $20 per week, reached by cab from port of Gananoque.
Provincial—N. McCarney, St. Lawrence River, 28 rooms, $2 per day, $7 to $10 per week, by cab.

BROCKVILLE.

St. Lawrence Hall—Amos Robinson, 200 rooms, $1.50 to $2 per day, $10.50 up per week, reached by ½ mile drive in hotel omnibus.
Revere House—J. C. Bann, 150 rooms, $2 to $2.50 per day, $10.50 to $14 per week, reached by 200 yards' drive in hotel omnibus.
Grand Central—S. Connor, 100 rooms, $1 to $1.50 per day, $5 to $9 per week, ¼ mile hotel bus.
Park—On river bank, above town, $1.50 per day, $8 up per week, 3 miles steamer from landing.

Numerous boarding houses for tourists, at reasonable rates; cottages may be rented along the banks of the river, within a few miles of the town.

PRESCOTT.

Daniels'—L. H. Daniels, 50 rooms, $2 to $3 per day, $7 to $14 per week, ⅛ mile omnibus or cab.
Revere—Wm. Cornell, 25 rooms, $1 to $1.50 per day, $6 per week, ⅛ mile omnibus or cab.

IROQUOIS.

Powell House—Jas. Powell, 15 rooms, $1.50 per day, $7 per week, 75 yards' walk or cab.

MORRISBURG.

St. Lawrence Hall—W. H. McGannon, 40 rooms, $1.50 per day, $8 to $8 per week, 200 yards cab.
Cottages may be rented at reasonable rates in the vicinity of Morrisburg.

CORNWALL.

Rossmore House—M. Ross, 65 rooms, $1.50 to $2 per day, $10.50 week, ¼ mile electric cars.

DICKINSON'S LANDING.

Conley House—Jas. Conley, Wales, 20 rooms, $1 per day, $5.50 per week, 1 mile omnibus.

COTEAU LANDING.

Tremont House—Alphonse Labelle, 12 rooms, 75c. to $1 per day, $3.50 to $4 per week, near port.

VALLEYFIELD.

La Roque House—Mrs. Monette, 30 rooms, $1.50 per day, near landing.
Windsor—Langlois, 30 rooms, $1.50 per day, near landing.

MONTREAL.

Windsor—W. S. Weldon, Dominion Square, 145 rooms, $3.50 to $5 per day, $21 up per week.
Balmoral—A. A. Welsh, Notre-Dame St., 250 rooms, $2 up per day, $21 per two weeks.
Queen's—C. & N. Vallée, corner Windsor and St. James Sts., 200 rooms, $2.50 to $3.50 per day, $14 up per week.
St. Lawrence Hall—H. Hogan, St. James St., 300 rooms, $2.50 up per day, $13 to $17 per week.
Place Viger—P. Poulin, 200 rooms, $3 to $4 per day American plan, $1.50 to $2 per day European plan, $21 per week, unlimited.
Riendeau—Jos. Riendeau, Jacques Cartier Square, 88 rooms, $1.50 to $2 per day.

Leading Hotels and Boarding Houses.

Jacques Cartier—J. B. Bureau, 15 rooms, $1.50 per day.
Turkish Bath—A. E. Newman, 63 St. Monique, 17 rooms, $1.75 to $2.50 p. day, $10 to $15 p. week.
Richelieu—F. B. Dumochel, St. Vincent St., 8 rooms, $2 to $3 p. day, European plan $1 up p. day.
Carslake—G. Carslake & Co., 572 St. James St., 50 rooms.
Albion—Peavey & Devlin, McGill St., 50 rooms, $2.50 to $3 per day, 1 mile drive from landing.
Stanley—A. Beliveau, Windsor St., 75 rooms, $1.50 to $3 per day.

These hotels are reached by ½ mile drive, omnibus, cabs, etc., from landing. Board may be obtained in private families in all parts of the city from $5 upwards.

SOREL.
Carleton—A. Lacocière, 35 rooms, $1.50 per day, near landing.
Brunswick—Nap. Lataverse, 15 rooms, $1.50 per day, near landing.

THREE RIVERS.
Dufresne—L. E. Dufresne, 25 rooms, $1.50 to $2.50 per day, $5 per week, 100 yards omnibus.
Dominion—Geo. Dufresne, 18 rooms, $1.50 per day, $8 per week, 100 yards drive in omnibus.
Windsor—J. Clontier, 28 rooms, $1 per day, $6 per week, 50 yards drive in omnibus.
Board with private families at reasonable rates.

BATISCAN.
Batiscan—T. Laguerre, 9 rooms, $1 per day, $4 to $5 per week, 135 yards from landing.

QUEBEC.
Chateau Frontenac—J. A. Beliveau, 200 rooms, $3.50 to $5 per day.
Victoria—Victoria Hotel Co., 45 rooms, $2 to $3 per day, $10 up per week.
Clarendon—Mrs. Pelletier, 60 rooms, $2 to $2.50 per day.
Mountain Hill House—E. Dion & Co., 65 rooms, $1 to $2 per day.

These hotels are reached by ½ mile drive, cabs, caleches or electric cars, from landing.

BAIE ST. PAUL.
Laroche—P. Laroche, 8 rooms, $1 per day, $6 per week, ½ mile from landing.
Cottages may be rented at from $15 to $20 per month, in good localities.

EBOULEMENTS.
Simon—Marc Simon, 7 rooms, 75c. per day, $5 per week, 1 mile from landing.

MURRAY BAY.
Lorne House—Wm. Chamard & Co., Pointe-à-Pic, P.Q., 100 rooms, $1.50 per day, $15 per month.
Warren's—N. Warren, Pointe-à-Pic, P.Q., 35 rooms, $1 to $1.50 per day, $30 to $40 per month.

These hotels are near the landing. A number of private boarding houses at $1 a day up.

CAP A-L'AIGLE.
Boarding House—J. Tremblay, 8 rooms, $1 per day, $5 per week, 1 mile from landing.
Boarding House—Mrs. Geo. Riverine, 18 rooms, $1 per day, $5 per week, 1 mile from landing.

RIVIÈRE-DU-LOUP.
Venise—L. T. Pnize, Fraserville, 8 rooms, $1.50 to $2 per day, $8 to $10 a week, 600 yards.
Bellevue—Aubut & Frère, Fraserville, 60 rooms, $1.50 to $2 per day, $8 to $10 per week, 100 yds.
Commercial—Geo. Gagnon, Rivière-du-Loup, 50 rooms, $1.50 per day, $7 to $10 per week, 1 mile.
Victoria—E. Gagnon, Rivière-du-Loup, 25 rooms, $1.50 per day, $7 to $8 per week.

TADOUSAC.
Tadousac—H. M. Patterson, 150 rooms, $2 to $3.50 per day, $12 to $15 per week, near landing.

HA HA BAY.
McLean's—35 rooms, $1 to $2 per day, near landing.

CHICOUTIMI.
Chateau Saguenay—Roméo Houle, 15 rooms, $2.50 to $5 per day, $12 to $25 per week.
Neron—Jos. Neron, 12 rooms, $1 per day, $5 per week.

Canadian General Electric Co.
Limited

Electrical Apparatus:

RAILWAY. POWER TRANSMISSION.
LIGHTING. MINING.

...ELECTRICAL SUPPLIES...

Head Office: TORONTO.

Factories: PETERBOROUGH, Ontario.

Branch Offices & Warerooms:

HALIFAX, MONTREAL, WINNIPEG, Man.,
VANCOUVER, ROSSLAND, B. C.

...Season of 1899...

United States Hotel,
SARATOGA SPRINGS, N.Y.

OPEN FROM JUNE 15 TO OCTOBER 1.

Special Rates for June, July and September.

For rates and other particulars, apply to

GAGE & PERRY.

CONGRESS SPRING

A Saline-Alkaline Water,
Cathartic and Alterative of High Medicinal Virtues.

As a Cathartic—One pint, or less, some thirty minutes before breakfast.
For Indigestion, Dyspepsia, Acid Stomach, Torpid Liver and inactive condition of the Kidneys—One third of a pint directly after each meal.
For Rheumatism, Malaria, Eczema, Scrofulous Taints, and all Diseases of the Blood—One quarter of a pint each time, and from four to six times a day.
For Insomnia—One half pint just before retiring acts as a *Sedative*, producing quiet sleep.

By its Efficacy, Purity and Acknowledged Sanitary properties, and the happy proportions of its various Alkaline Salts, the CONGRESS stands unrivalled by all foreign or domestic waters.

FOR SALE BY REPUTABLE DRUGGISTS, WINE MERCHANTS AND HOTELS.
AND
Congress Spring Co., Saratoga Springs, N.Y.

The Arlington Hotel, Toronto, Having accommodation for persons, is most centrally located, being only three blocks from Union Station and only ten minutes walk to theatres and places of interest. Car lines pass in front of Hotel, affording transportation facilities to all parts of the city. The Hotel is under new management, Mr. C. J. BEACHAM being the capable and popular managing director.
Rates are from $2.00, $2.50 to $3.00 per day.

→Hotel · Victoria←
---QUEBEC---

A Delightful Hotel for Tourists while visiting the old Fortress City.

One Block from the Grand Battery.
Overlooking the Beautiful Valley of the St. Charles River.
A Picturesque Panorama of Beauty and Grandeur.

Rooms with Bath and en suite.
Turkish, Russian, Electric and Swimming Baths connected with Hotel.

RATES: $2.00 TO $3.00 PER DAY.

St. Lawrence Hall,

CACOUNA, P. Q.

CANADA.

This elegant and spacious hotel, situated at the beautiful and fashionable Canadian watering place on the Lower St. Lawrence, one hundred and twenty miles below Quebec, opposite the mouth of the far-famed Saguenay River, is open from June to September.

CACOUNA is a great natural sanitarium. Its salubrity, elevation and average summer temperature, as well as salt sea breezes and balmy air, make it specially attractive. The strong air produces sweet sleep and perfect rest. Sea Bathing, Cycling, Boating, Sailing, Athletics, Dancing, Concerts, etc.

PRICES For transient, $2 to $3 per day, $0 and upwards per week, according to location of rooms. Special rates for families for the season.

Cacouna is reached by Richelieu and Ontario Navigation Company's Steamers from Rivière-du-Loup wharf, or by Intercolonial Railway from Cacouna Station.

Ask for illustrated pamphlet, with diagram of the Hall.

JOHN BRENNAN,
Manager.

"And the night went down, and the sun smiled out far over the summer sea,
And the Spanish fleet with broken sides lay round us all in a ring;
But they dared not touch us again, for they feared that we still could sting."

The Revenge A ballad of the fleet.

Did you ever see a "Ouananiche"?

. . . ON VIEW AT

" The Sportsman's Paradise,"
11 St. John Street.

Information as to Ouananiche, Salmon and
Trout Fishing How and where
to get them.

GREGORY'S FLY REPELLENT.

VAN'S SPECIALTIES:

The most complete stock in
Canada of .

**Fishing Tackle, Hunting Outfits and
Sportsmen's Requisites.**

Canoes, Tents, Cavp Fittings, &c.
*Guides secured.
Provisions to order.
Bicycles and Accessories.
Guns, Rifles, Ammunitions.*

THE V. &. B. SPORTING GOODS STORE,
QUEBEC, P. Q.

Telephone 190. P. O. Box 1059.

QUEBEC STEAMSHIP CO., LTD.

Bermuda and West India Lines.

NEW YORK and BERMUDA ROYAL MAIL STEAMSHIP LINE.
The "A1" Iron Steamship "TRINIDAD," 3,000 tons, or "ORINOCO," 2,000 tons, specially built for the route, having the newest and best passenger accommodation, sail from the Company's pier 47, North River, New York, every five days, from January to June, and every ten days thereafter.

NEW YORK and WINDWARD ISLANDS MAIL STEAMSHIP LINE.
St. Thomas, St. Croix, St. Kitts, Antigua, Gaudeloupe, Dominica, Martinique, St. Lucia, Barbados :—The First-class Iron Steamships "PRETORIA," 3,300 tons, "MADIANA," 3,100 tons, "FONTABELLE," 2,700 tons, "CARIBBEE," 2,000 tons, with excellent passenger accommodation, are scheduled to sail from pier 47, North River, New York, alternately *every ten days.*

Special Cruises to the WEST INDIES during January, February and March.

ST. LAWRENCE LINE TO MARITIME PROVINCES.
The Twin Screw Iron Steamship "CAMPANA," 1,700 tons, having the latest modern passenger accommodations, will sail from Montreal for Picton, N.S., calling at Quebec, Father Point, Gaspé, Malbaie, Percé, Summerside, Charlottetown, and Souris, P.E.I., every alternate Monday, at 2 p.m., during the season of navigation, sailing from Quebec the following Tuesdays at noon. At Picton the Intercolonial Railway train is taken for Halifax, whence connections can be made for St. John's, Nfld., St. John, N.B., Portland, Boston and New York.

For all information as to the above routes, apply to

THOMAS COOK & SON, General Ticket Agents, 261 & 262 Broadway, New York.
J. G. BROCK, Agent, 211 Commissioners Street, Montreal.
A. E. OUTERBRIDGE & CO., Agents, 39 Broadway, New York.
or to **ARTHUR AHERN,** Secretary, Quebec, Canada.

THE "RUSSELL"

F. X. St-Jacques,
PROPRIETOR.

**OTTAWA,
CANADA.**

Patterson-Paisley Hotel Circuit.

THE NEW ROYAL, THE LEADING HOTEL, HAMILTON, CAN.
Rates: $2.50 to $4.00 per day. American plan.

THE PENETANGUISHENE,
CANADA'S GREAT SUMMER HOTEL.
Beautifully situated on the Georgian Bay. Excellent boating, bathing and fishing. Electric light, steam heat and all modern improvements.
Rates: $2.00 and $2.50 per day, $10.00 to $15.00 per week. Special rates for families.

HOTEL SANS SOUCI.
Situated at the mouth of the Moon River, Georgian Bay, on the route of the North Shore Navigation Co.; the "City of Toronto" calling with mail and passengers twice daily.
The greatest fishing and hunting grounds in the Muskoka District. Black Bass and Maskinongé in abundance.
A new hotel with all modern conveniences, enamelled baths, etc. Steam launch, row boats and guides can be secured at the hotel.

THE BELVIDERE, PARRY SOUND, ONT.
The most picturesquely situated hotel on the Georgian Bay.

PATTERSON & PAISLEY,
Write for Booklets.   Proprietors.

How to See Niagara Falls.

Niagara Falls Park and River Railway....
The Greatest Scenic Trolley Route in the World.

THE tourist has a magnificent view from the observation cars of this road of the upper rapids, the Horseshoe and the American Falls, the Gorge, the Whirlpool Rapids, the Whirlpool and Lower River Rapids, the great Bridges which span the Gorge, Queenston Heights, Brock's Monument, the battlefield of Chippewa and other historic spots along the river, the marvellous Niagara Glen and picturesque ravines, a variety of scenery unsurpassed in beauty and grandeur.

Fare, Round Trip, 75 cents.
A distance of 25 miles.

A ferry connects with New York Central trains and Gorge Road cars at Lewiston to Queenston, where the cars of the Niagara Falls Park & River Road are waiting.
For further information, address

W. PHILLIPS, *General Manager,*
NIAGARA FALLS, Ont.

OPPOSITE
CITY HALL
SQUARE.

H. ALEXANDER,
PROPRIETOR.

Riendeau Hotel,

Opposite Court House and City Hall.

Nos. 58 & 60
Jacques Cartier Square,
MONTREAL.

D. MORGAN,
Tailor.

The Pink of Fashion
FOR

LADIES' TAILOR:
Costumes,
Habits,
New Markets,
Jackets,
Golf Capes.

GENTS' TAILOR.
Overcoatings,
Suiting,
Vesting,
Trousering,
London Ready-Made Clothing.

☞ All goods made on the shortest notice with care.

☞ Remember "The Maine" Establishment for the best and lowest quotations.

D. MORGAN, QUEBEC.

OTTAWA, CAN

The Windsor,
OTTAWA,
CANADA.

Further Enlargement of 40 Rooms.

Rates graduated according to location of room.

Advertisements.

The....

Queen's Hotel,

...Toronto, Ont.

McGAW & WINNETT, Proprietors.

ONE of the Largest and Most Comfortable Hotels in the Dominion of Canada, being adjacent to the Lake, commands splendid view of Toronto Bay and Lake Ontario. It is well known as one of the Coolest Houses, in Summer, in Canada, and is elegantly furnished throughout. Rooms *en suite*, with bath rooms attached, on every floor.

The Queen's has been liberally patronized by Royalty and nobility during their visits to Toronto, and among those who have honored it with their patronage are :

His Imperial Highness, the Grand Duke Alexis of Russia.	**The Earl and Countess of Dufferin.**
Their Royal Highnesses, Prince Leopold, Prince George, Princess Louise, and the Duke and Duchess of Connaught.	**The Marquis and Marchioness of Lansdowne.**
	Lord and Lady Stanley of Preston.
	The Earl and Countess of Aberdeen.
The Marquis of Lorne.	**Lord and Lady Minto,**
	and the Best Families.

THE QUEEN'S is furnished with all the Latest Modern Improvements. Handsome Passenger Elevator, Electric Bells, etc.

THE QUEEN'S is but three stories high, covering a large area of ground, used exclusively for hotel purposes, and having lawns on either side, with means of exit from the house, in addition to those in front and rear ; these render it almost impossible for any accident to take place from fire, consequently THE QUEEN'S is looked upon as the safest hotel in the Dominion of Canada.

Telephone Communication to all parts.   **No Runners employed.**

Privy Council Chamber, Ottawa.

The Canadian Rubber Co.
OF MONTREAL.

 . . MANUFACTURERS OF . .
**RUBBER BOOTS AND SHOES,
FELT OVERSHOES,
LUMBERMEN'S GUM SHOES,**
. . AND . .
FINE-CLASS FOOTWEAR,
ALSO,
**BELTING, PACKING, HOSE,
CLOTHING, Etc.**

Offices and Warerooms:
MONTREAL, TORONTO AND WINNIPEG.
Factory:
PAPINEAU SQUARE, MONTREAL.

Furness  Lines...

DIRECT FORTNIGHLY SERVICE
BETWEEN
HALIFAX, N. S., AND LONDON.

The fast, full-powered, high-class Clyde built Steamships:

"**London City,**"   3000 tons. Captain Paterson.
"**Halifax City,**" 3000 tons, Captain Newton.
"**St. John City,**" 3000 tons, Captain Campbell.

Will sail, weather and circumstances permitting, every alternate Thursday, from Halifax, N. S., to London, G. B. Rates of passage, $45.00 to $60.00, according to position of berth.

FORTNIGHLY SERVICE
BETWEEN
HALIFAX, N.S., & LIVERPOOL
Via *ST. JOHN'S*, *Newfoundland*.

The fast, full-powered, high-class Clyde built Steamships:

"**Dahome,**" 3000 tons, Captain Forth.
"**Damara,**" 3000 tons, Captain Williams.
"**Ulunda,**" 3000 tons, Captain Fleming.

Will sail, weather and circumstances permitting, every alternate Wednesday, from Halifax, N. S., to Liverpool, G. B., via St. John's, Newfoundland. Rates of passage, $45.00 to $50.00, according to position of berth.

These steamers have superior accommodation for first-class passengers and carry a stewardess. London steamers carry a doctor. The saloon and sleeping berths being well ventilated and placed amidships, secure for passengers that greatest luxury at sea—fresh air, with the minimum of motion. Special through rate from Montreal to London or Liverpool, $55.00 to $60.00, according to position of berth.

Gentlemen's Smoke Room. Electrically lighted throughout.

The steamers *St. John City* and *Halifax City* are fitted with cold storage chambers for conveyance of Fresh Meats, Butter, Cheese, Fruit and other classes of goods for which cold storage is desirable.

For sailing dates and terms of freight apply to

FURNESS, WITHY & CO., Ltd., Agents.
People's Bank Buildings, HALIFAX.

Gardens at Weston.

BARTON BROS.

Wholesale and Retail
Dealers in

Fruit, Vegetables, and Flowers.

We work 90 acres of Garden land in Weston.

Goods shipped by Rail and Boat.

20 & 22 ST. LAWRENCE MARKET,
TORONTO.

Telephone No. 2688.

JOHN MALLON & CO.

Meat Market.

We have the best facilities for handling large accounts.

*Railroads,
Steamboats,
Public Institutions,
Hotels, etc.*

MESS BEEF supplied on short notice at lowest prices.

St. Lawrence Market,
TORONTO.

Telephone 651.

Royal Oil Co.,

TORONTO
AND MONTREAL.

THE LARGEST OIL FIRM IN CANADA.

ILLUMINATING,
CYLINDER,
ENGINE and
DYNAMO

ORDERS APPRECIATED.

Please ask for Samples and Quotations.

I. X. L.
Steam Laundry Company.

J. GARDNER, Proprietor.

78 Queen Street West,

A few doors West of New Court House.

...**TORONTO.**

Telephone 2402.

Balmoral Hotel

A. ARCH. WELSH,
Proprietor.

NOTRE-DAME ST., MONTREAL.

The BALMORAL is the finest down-town hotel in the city of Montreal. Only two blocks from the magnificent Cathedral, on the great artery of trade, Notre-Dame street. Special attention and rates to excursion parties.

American plan, $2.00 to $4.00 per day.
European plan, $1.00 and upwards.

The...
Algonquin.

The best Summer Hotel on the St. Lawrence is situated on Stanley Island, midway in the course of the Richelieu and Ontario Nav. Co's route of travel from Toronto to Chicoutimi.

It has for several years been the favorite resort of the summer visitor, the sportsman and the tourist.

The Fishing and Shooting are unsurpassed, while the attractions for summer outing, including boating, outdoor and indoor amusements are unexcelled.

For terms and particulars and free illustrated booklet apply to

J. R. DUQUETTE,
Stanley Island,
SUMMERSTOWN P. O., Ont.

All the Finest
Passenger and Freight Steamers
on the Great Lakes
are equipped with

...The...
FULLER DYNAMOS
AND
SHIP SIGNAL APPARATUS.

THE FULLER COMPANY, DETROIT, MICH., U.S.A.

Fuller Dynamos.
Fuller Motors.
Fuller Fans.

Steel Plate Blowers
for Forced Draft.

...The...
Polson Iron Works
TORONTO.

Engines and Boilers, Steel Vessels FOR EVERY SERVICE.

BUILDERS IN CANADA OF THE

YARROW & MOSHER Patent Water-Tube Boilers.

Works and Office: ESPLANADE EAST, TORONTO.

The Toronto Silver Plate Co., Ltd.

SILVERSMITHS AND MANUFACTURERS
...OF...

Electro Silver Plate.

No. 662—Tea Pot.

MAKE A SPECIALTY OF SILVERWARE FOR

HOTEL, CLUB, DINING CAR AND STEAMBOAT USE.

No. 672 —Coffee Pot.

Factories and Salesrooms: **KING ST. WEST, TORONTO, Can.**

E. G. GOODERHAM, Manager and Sec.-Treasurer.

...Established 1864...

DANIELS' HOTEL

L. H. DANIELS,
Proprietor.

...PRESCOTT, ONT.

... Rebuilt in 1884, at a cost of $10,000 ...

First class in all its appointments. Spacious Parlors, Pleasant and Cheerful Sleeping Rooms, Magnificent Billiard Hall and Fine Sample Rooms. Electric Bells throughout the House, and lighted by Electricity.

SANITARIAN ARRANGEMENTS UNSURPASSED.

The Block adjoining is now added, and the DANIELS' is now one of the largest and most complete Hotels in Canada.

Travellers visiting the Capital, only 54 miles distant, or those desiring a day's lay-off, will find every comfort and convenience at this well managed hotel.

Furniture and Upholstery.

IN STOCK.

The largest selection in Canada of Fine and Medium Priced Furniture, including Brass and Enamelled Bedsteads, from the best English and American makers.

TO ORDER.

Everything in Cabinet Work, including Furniture, Mantels and Interior Woodwork, for examples of which see the magnificent fittings of the new steamer "Toronto" on this Line.

The CHAS. ROGERS & SONS CO., Limited,
97 Yonge Street, TORONTO.

The Royal Electric Company

MONTREAL, QUE.

WESTERN OFFICE:
TORONTO, ONT.

MANUFACTURERS OF

ELECTRICAL MACHINERY AND APPARATUS

. . FOR . .

Incandescent Lighting,	Power Transmission,
Arc Lighting,	Mill Work,
Electric Railways,	Electrical Mining.

SOLE MAKERS FOR CANADA OF THE **S.K.C. TWO-PHASE SYSTEM**

of Alternating-Current Generators, Motors and Transformers,

DISTANT WATER POWERS UTILIZED FOR ALL CLASSES OF WORK. by means of which Incandescent Lights, Arc Lights and Power can be served from the same dynamo and the same current.

Hotel Empire,
Broadway (formerly Boulevard), and 63d Street, New York City.

Conducted on the AMERICAN and EUROPEAN PLANS, for the accommodation of those who want the best at reasonable cost.

Electric cars to all parts of the city pass its doors Sixth and Ninth Ave. Elevated Railway stations one minute's walk from the hotel.

Within ten minutes of all the principal Theatres and Great Department Stores.

A Perfect Home, alike for the Tourist and Business Man.

An extensive library of choice literature has just been added.

Orchestral Concert Every Evening.

From all Jersey City ferries take the Sixth or Ninth Avenue Elevated trains to 59th Street, or Broadway cable to Hotel door, in 20 minutes.

Take Boulevard cars at Grand Central Depot and reach HOTEL EMPIRE in 7 minutes.

At the EMPIRE you get luxury and comfort for what it ordinarily costs to live at inferior hotels.

Rates Moderate.

EXCLUSIVE, MODERN, FIREPROOF

Write for our book: "THE EMPIRE ILLUSTRATED."

W. JOHNSON QUINN, PROPRIETOR.

Davis Dry Dock Company,
Docking and Repairing of all kinds.

We make a specialty of building all kinds of Steam Yachts from 20 ft. up to 200 ft.

Cut of 20 Foot Family Steam Launch "Little Comfort," Speed 6 miles an hour.

DAVIS & SONS, Builders,
KINGSTON, Ont.

Tents all Sizes for Hire.
Camping Outfits, Oil Clothing, etc., etc.

MONTREAL TENT, AWNING AND TARPAULIN CO.
W. H. GRIFFIN, Manager.

249 & 251 Commissioners Street, Montreal.
Telephone, Main 2455.

Rideau Canal, Ottawa, Ont.

Premo Camera,

BEST FOR THE TOURIST.

OWING to its extreme compactness, the Pony **PREMO** is especially adapted for the use of all Sportsmen. Just think of a complete 4 x 5 Camera, measuring only 2 x 5 x 6 inches, and weighing but two pounds.

ROCHESTER OPTICAL CO.,

SEND FOR PREMO PAMPHLET
GIVING FULL PARTICULARS.

ROCHESTER, N.Y.

The Cleveland and Buffalo Transit Company,

Conne ting Cleveland and Buffalo while you sleep.

DAILY LINE BETWEEN

Buffalo Cleveland and Toledo.

Owning and operating the Finest, Largest, Fastest and Most Modern Steel, Side-wheel Steamers on the Great Lakes.

"City of Erie" (new) "City of Buffalo" (new)
"State of New York" "State of Ohio"

Ask any Coupon Ticket Agent in the United States or Canada for Tickets via C. & B. Line. Direct Connections made at Buffalo and Cleveland with all rail lines.

Send two 2-cent stamps for illustrated pamphlet to

W. F. HERMAN,
General Passenger Agent,
CLEVELAND, Ohio.

Steamers of this Company operate from April 1st to December 1st each year.

COMFORT IN TRAVEL.

Chicago to New York,
Boston and the East.

THE GREAT SUMMER TOURIST ROUTE

to Niagara Falls,
The Thousand Islands,
Rapids of the St. Lawrence,
The Adirondacks,   Green Mountains,
White Mountains,
and New England Coast.

During the Summer Season the Through Car Service will be extended to all the Principal Resorts.

For full information and illustrated folders, address:

L. D. HEUSNER,   O. W. RUGGLES,
General Western Passenger Agent.   General Passenger and Ticket Agent.
CHICAGO.   CHICAGO.

The Northern Transit Co.,

SEMI-WEEKLY BETWEEN

**TOLEDO,   DETROIT,   CLEVELAND,   TORONTO,
OSWEGO,   ALEXANDRIA BAY,
THE THOUSAND ISLANDS,   OGDENSBURG and PRESCOTT.**

Steamer "Empire State," 1000 tons.
Steamer "Badger State," 1000 tons.

Lighted by electricity and having all the latest appliances for the safety and comfort of passengers. Connecting at ALEXANDRIA BAY with steamers of the Richelieu & Ontario Navigation Company, for MONTREAL, QUEBEC and SAGUENAY RIVER.

For further information, circulars, etc., address:

FARASEY & MARRON, GENERAL AGENTS,
OR **W. A. COLLIER**, GENERAL MANAGER.
CLEVELAND, OHIO.

Five Interesting Numbers

... of the ...

"Four-Track Series"

The New York Central's Books of Travel

No. 22

" Saratoga the Beautiful "

Highly embellished with seventy-five new and beautiful half-tone illustrations and entertaining text.

No. 25

"A Message to Garcia"

A preachment that every young man and young woman in the land should read and commit to memory.

No. 8

"Two to Fifteen Days' Pleasure Tours "

Containing maps, routes, rates, and time required for more than one hundred delightful vacation tours.

No. 6

" In the Adirondack Mountains "

Illustrating and describing the wonderful Adirondack region. Contains list of hotels, lakes, and large maps.

No. 16

"Illustrated Catalogue of the Four-Track Series "

is the New York Central's book of books for travelers. In addition to a brief review of the various books and etchings comprised in the series, it contains a half-tone reproduction on a small scale of the title-page of each book and the subject of the etching.

Either of the above books will be sent free, post-paid, to any address upon receipt of a 2-cent stamp, or the Catalogue for a 1-cent stamp, by George H. Daniels, General Passenger Agent, Grand Central Station, New York.

Advertisements.

Dominion Line Royal Mail Steamships.

FAST AND LARGE STEAMERS—WEEKLY SAILINGS

MONTREAL and QUEBEC to LIVERPOOL.

Cambroman, 5,000 tons.   Vancouver, 5,000.   Ottoman, 5,000 tons.
Dominion, 6,500 tons.   Scotsman, 6,000 tons.
Twin Screw.   Twin Screw.

SALOONS AND STATEROOMS AMIDSHIPS.

Superior accommodation for all classes of passengers at moderate rates. One thousand miles of river and gulf smooth water sailing, after leaving Montreal, before the Atlantic is reached, making a very short sea passage.

BOSTON SERVICE   BOSTON TO LIVERPOOL VIA QUEENSTOWN.

SS. Canada, 9,000 tons.   SS. New England, 11,600 tons.
Twin Screw.   Twin Screw.
SS. Derbyshire, 7,000 tons.
Twin Screw.

Palace Steamers of great speed, having all the appointments of a first-class hotel. Carrying the United States mail.
For further particulars, apply to any local agent of the Company, or

RICHARDS, MILLS & CO.,   **DAVID TORRANCE & CO.,**
103 State St., Boston,   *General Agents,*
or 69 Dearborn St., Chicago.   *Montreal.*

Quebec Central Ry.   The ... Tourist Route.

...BETWEEN...

QUEBEC, PORTLAND, BOSTON & NEW YORK.

...Through Fast Express Trains...

Pullman Parlor Cars on day trains and Sleeping Cars on night trains.
Solid train service between Quebec and Boston without change.
The most direct route between Quebec and all New England and New York points is *via* the Quebec Central Railway, Sherbrooke and Boston & Maine R.R.
The favorite route for Tourists from Quebec to Portland and all Maine points is *via* Quebec Central Railway, Dudswell Jct. and Maine Central R.R., passing through the heart of the White Mountains.

Ask for tickets *via* the Quebec Central Railway, and for full information, time tables, etc., apply to

R. M. STOCKING,   **FRANK GRUNDY,**   **J H. WALSH,**
CITY & DISTRICT AGENT.   GENERAL MANAGER.   GEN'L PASS. AGENT,
QUEBEC. P.Q.   SHERBROOKE. P.Q.   SHERBROOKE, P.Q.

The JOHN L. CASSIDY CO., Ltd.

MANUFACTURERS AND IMPORTERS OF

CHINA, SILVERWARE,
CROCKERY, CUTLERY,
GLASSWARE. LAMPS, ETC.

OFFICES AND WAREHOUSE:

339 & 341 St. Paul Street,

CITY BRANCHES:

235 St. Lawrence Main Street,
1471 St. Catherine Street, East.
2503 St. Catherine Street, West.

MONTREAL.

...SMOKE...

"Chamberlain"

..AND..

"Lafayette"

CIGARS.

J. M. FORTIER,

Manufacturer,

MONTREAL.

PURE ICE.

The City Ice Co.
Limited,

R. A. BECKET,
Manager.

26 Victoria Square.

Pure Ice and prompt delivery.

Capacity, 50,000 tons.

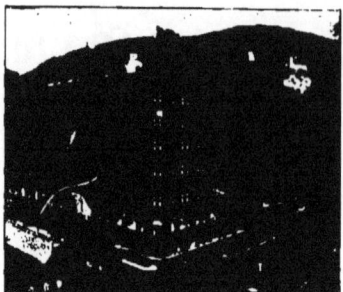

Queen's Hotel,
MONTREAL.

The only Fire-proof Hotel in the city.

STRICTLY FIRST-CLASS.

C. & N. VALLEE, PROPRIETORS.   GEO. D. FUCHS, MANAGER.

W. HENRY, MANAGER. MONTREAL. LIMITED.

McKelvey & Birch,

Tinsmiths, Bell Hangers, Plumbers, Steam Fitters, and Coppersmiths,

69 and 71 Brock Street, Kingston.

HUDON, HÉBERT & CO.

Wholesale Grocers
...and...
..Wine Importers..

**Montreal,**

41 St. Sulpice Street,   Canada.
and 22 de Brosoles Street.

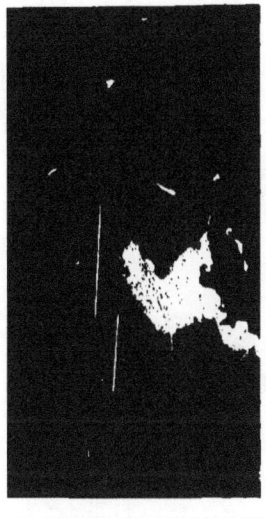

J. & R. WEIR,

Steel Boat Builders, Engineers, Boilermakers, and Machinists.

NAZARETH & BRENNAN STS.,

MONTREAL.

Drink...

TIMMONS'

Ginger Ale, Soda Water, Ciderine, Lemonade, etc.

QUEBEC.

Medals, First Prizes and Diplomas awarded for Superior Quality.

St. Johns, P.Q.

The Iroquois

HORSMAN & CO.
PROPRIETORS.

Corner King and York Streets,

Most Modern Hotel in the City.   TORONTO, CANADA.

CENTRALLY LOCATED.

Rooms with Bath and all Modern Improvements.

AMERICAN AND EUROPEAN PLAN.

...TOURISTS WELL TAKEN CARE OF...

••"WE LEAD, LET THOSE WHO CAN, FOLLOW."••

J. H. BRADLEY, Prescott, Ont.

DEALER IN

Fine Groceries, Crockery and Table Delicacies, Fruit and Vegetables, Etc.

Special attention given to Supplying of Boats.

TELEPHONE 36.

GANANOQUE ON THE ST. LAWRENCE.

The Gananoque Inn,

A. L. FULLER, Proprietor.

The Best Accommodation

FOR GUESTS of any hotel on the St. Lawrence. Every modern convenience.

Wide Halls, Spacious Parlors and Verandas, Bath Rooms, Electric Lights and Bells. Elevators.

Warmed on chilly mornings and evenings by Hot Water.

Plumbing and Heating the Best.

Rooms large and commanding beautiful views

Cuisine Unsurpassed.
Rates Reasonable.

IF YOU COME, YOU WILL STAY.

THE BEST FISHING
on the River is in sight from the Porch of "The Gananoque Inn."

The view of the ADMIRALTY GROUP OF ISLANDS, *the most picturesque in the river*, is had from THE INN Porch and windows.

BOAT LIVERIES AND SKILLED FISHERMEN.

The Imperial Oil Co.,
Limited.

LUBRICATING
ILLUMINATING **OILS**

GREASES.
NAPTHA.

124, 126 & 128
Board of Trade Building,
MONTREAL.

Bell Telephone, Main 2772 & 2903.
Merchants Telephone, 870.

MOTTO: "THE BEST."

On the boat and at all stopping places ask for

GURD'S

GINGER ALE,
SODA WATER,
APPLE NECTAR,
CREAM SODA,
KOLA, Etc., Etc.

Also note that Caledonian leads all Natural Mineral Waters.

7 Gold, 7 Silver and 5 Bronze Medals Awarded for Excellence.

CHARLES GURD & CO.,
MONTREAL.

The New Frontenac,
Round Island,
Thousand Islands,
St. Lawrence River, N. Y.

Opens June 20.

Enlarged to twice its former capacity, contains over 300 rooms, more than half of them en suite, with private bath rooms. **Entirely refitted** with new and elegant furnishings, a **new Dining Room, 65 x 100 feet,** and new kitchens with every device known to modern art for perfection in cooking. Fresh vegetables, milk, cream, butter and eggs supplied daily from the Hotel farm.

CUISINE AND SERVICE UNEXCELLED.

Café, Billiard parlors, Bowling, Tennis and an **exceptionally fine nine hole Golf course,** which will be in the charge of an experienced greens keeper.

As fine Fishing and Boating as the heart could desire.

For circulars, terms, etc., address:

M. C. WENTWORTH, Manager.

Geo. Wentworth is also proprietor of Wentworth Hall and Cottages, Jackson, White Mountains, N. H.

A. Grenier, TEL. 241

GROCER and WINE MERCHANT

Supplies for Fishing and Hunting Clubs

..A SPECIALTY..

ALSO AGENT FOR

Pabst Brewing Co's Milwaukee Lager Beer.

49 ST. JOHN STREET,
..QUEBEC..

FACTORY: 44 Ursule St.,
CENTRAL OFFICE: 324 St. John Street,
QUEBEC.

Frontenac Electric Laundry

This establishment has been re-organized and equipped with Electric Power and Modern Machinery, and has a capacity of 20,000 pieces a day.

Patronized by all the Nobility and Gentry from all parts of the Dominion, Trans-atlantic Royal Mail Steamers, and Canadian Pacific.

ALL WORK GUARANTEED
PROMPT DESPATCH.

SPECIAL RATES MADE WITH OCEAN AND GULF STEAMERS.

G. BLAKE,
Manager.

Telephone 410.

HOTEL JACQUES CARTIER

J. B. BUREAU & CO.,
PROPRIETORS.

19, 21, 23, 25
PLACE
JACQUES CARTIER
MONTREAL.

Rates: $1 25 to $2 00
per day
ACCORDING TO LOCATION

AMERICAN AND EUROPEAN PLANS.

BELL TEL MAIN 1117. Close to Depots, Boat Landings and Street Cars.

Closing and binding the tick.

OSTERMOOR'S
Patent Elastic
Felt Mattress.

Closing and binding the tick.

$15.00 FULL DOUBLE SIZE.

Its advantages :
   Will not mat or pack down ;
   Never requires teasing or remaking ;
   An occasional sun-bath keeps it ever new ;
   Is made of absolutely pure, snow-white, elastic material ;
   Is purer than the best curled horse hair at half its price ;

A post-card with your name will bring you our illustrated booklet telling all about this marvellous bed.

Closing and binding the tick.

THE ALASKA FEATHER AND
DOWN CO., Ltd.

290 Guy Street - - **MONTREAL.**

Closing and binding the tick.

Ottawa River Navigation Company.

DAY  *Modern*
MAIL LINE. *Steel Steamers.*

. . BETWEEN . .

OTTAWA AND MONTREAL.

STEAMERS "SOVEREIGN," "EMPRESS," "DUCHESS OF YORK."

LEAVE OTTAWA 7.30 A.M.
LEAVING MONTREAL, PASSENGERS TAKE G.T.R. 8 A.M. TRAIN FOR LACHINE TO CONNECT WITH STEAMERS FOR OTTAWA.

Panorama of Scenic Beauty the Whole Way.

SHOOTING THE LACHINE RAPIDS.

Steamers go alongside Richelieu & Ontario Navigation Co.'s Steamers to transfer Passengers for Quebec and Lower St. Lawrence.

Head Office: 161, 163 and 165 Common St. *R. W. SHEPHERD,*
MONTREAL. *Man.-Director.*

NIAGARA RIVER LINE.

··▶ ◀··

Niagara Navigation Company, Limited,
TORONTO, CANADA.

THE SHORT AND PICTURESQUE ROUTE BETWEEN

BUFFALO, NIAGARA FALLS & TORONTO.

The only line giving passengers views of Falls, Rapids, Brock's Monument and the romantic scenery of the lower Niagara.

Season opens about May 15th; closes about October 10th.

Connections at foot of Rapids with New York Central R.R. and Niagara Falls & Lewiston R.R. (Electric) on American side, and Michigan Central R.R. and Niagara Falls Park R.R. on Canadian side. Connections at Toronto with the Richelieu and Ontario Navigation Co.'s steamers, the Canadian Pacific Railway and the Grand Trunk System.

Tickets at all offices of New York Central Lines and principal offices in Niagara Falls and Toronto.

H W. GARTH. J. H. GARTH

GARTH & CO.

ESTABLISHED 1828.

Brass & Iron Founders,
Hot Water and Steam Engineers, Plumbers.

MANUFACTURERS OF
Gas and Electric Light Fixtures, Fire and Water Department Supplies, Iron, Brass and Copper Castings.

IMPORTERS OF
Wrought and Cast Iron Pipes, Malleable and Cast Iron Fittings, Sanitary Earthenware, Lavatory Fittings, Etc.

AGENTS AND MANUFACTURERS FOR

Penberthy Injectors.
Korting Injectors.
Fellow's Little Giant and Twin Comet Lawn Sprinklers.
Beaton's Perfection Floor Plates.
Michigan Lubricators.
Trimont Manufacturing Company.
Brock's Chain Pipe Wrenches.
King's Flue Scrapers.
Foster's Pressure Regulators and Pump Governors.
Vanclasen's Steam Jet Pumps.
Newton's Sanitary Traps.
Braender's Jet Pumps and Water Elevators.
Cornell's Self-Closing Basin Faucets.

Giepel's Patent Steam Traps.
National Meter Co.'s Water Meters.
Buckeye Bell Foundry Co.'s Bells.
Watson's Pressure Regulators.
Jenkins Bros.' Valves.
Wilhelmi Copper Boilers.
Curtis' Pressure Regulators.
Pierce, Butler & Pierce's Non-Drip Air Valves.
Fairbanks' Asbestos Packed Cocks.
McDaniel's Exhaust Heads, Steam Traps and Suction Tees.
Bernard & Frank's Bath and Bedroom Trimmings.
Moncrieff's Gauge Glasses.

536 TO 542 CRAIG STREET.

IRON FOUNDRY:
CORNER MAISONNEUVE & LAGAUCHETIERE STS
MONTREAL.

TELEPHONES: OFFICE, MAIN 319. FOUNDRY, EAST 422.

Send for Catalogues and Price Lists.

Advertisements.

BETTER BEER WAS NEVER BREWED

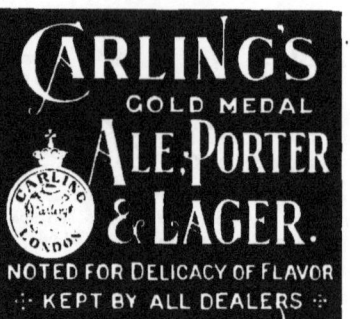

A PERFECT TONIC FOR TOURISTS

AS a holiday beverage CARLING'S ALE is without an equal. Bright, sparkling and healthful, it is an ideal tonic and a pleasing drink.

CARLING'S ALE and PORTER is for sale on all Richelieu and Ontario Navigation Co.'s boats and can be procured from nearly every liquor dealer in Canada.

THESE LABELS ON A BOTTLE OF ALE OR PORTER ARE AN ABSOLUTE GUARANTEE THAT THE CONTENTS ARE PURE, SOUND AND PERFECTLY MATURED.

The Carling B. & M. Co.
Limited,
London, Canada.

WE ONLY WANT JUSTICE

ONE OF THE LEADING ATTRACTIONS OF THE LOWER ST. LAWRENCE, ACCIDENTALLY LEFT OUT OF THE OFFICIAL LIST, IS

THE GREAT MANUFACTURING PLANT OF **CARRIER, LAINE & CO.,** DIRECTLY OPPOSITE "THE OLD ROCK CITY," QUEBEC. **LEVIS, QUE.**

A glance from the steamer's deck in our direction will repay you.

If you are thinking of having a Steam Launch or a Steamboat built, or of purchasing Engines, Boilers, Mill Machinery, Cheese Factory or Creamery Outfits, High-grade Ranges and Stoves.

It will pay you to stop over.

No matter what your wants are in the line of Machinery, we are in a better position than any firm in Canada to supply you.

EXCLUSIVE STYLES
AND MATERIALS ....

J. J. MILLOY,

FASHIONABLE TAILOR

FOR
GENTLEMEN
AND LADIES.

2301 & 2303 ST. CATHERINE ST.,

GENTLEMEN'S SUITS AND LADIES' COSTUMES
TO ORDER ON SHORT NOTICE TO ACCOMODATE
TRANSIENT VISITORS.

MONTREAL.

www.ingramcontent.com/pod-product-compliance
Lightning Source LLC
Chambersburg PA
CBHW031446160426
43195CB00010BB/872